CIRCLES OF CHANGE

CIRCLES OF CHANGE

VOLUME I

An Adventure in Therapeutic Community at Atascadero State Hospital

Joseph Abrahams, M.D.

IPBOOKS.net
International Psychoanalytic Books

International Psychoanalytic Books (IPBooks)
New York • http://www.IPBooks.net

Published by International Psychoanalytic Books (IPBooks)
Queens, New York
Online at: www.IPBooks.net

Book cover design by Kathy Kovacic

Interior book design by Medlar Publishing Solutions Pvt Ltd., India

www.IPBooks.net

ISBN: 978-1-949093-20-9

Table of Contents

Preface

Circles of Change represents the culmination of Dr. Abrahams' seven-decade career as a psychoanalyst. In this two-volume book he comes full circle from his roots as one of the creative leaders of American institutional psychiatry, starting at Fort Knox Military Prison and St. Elizabeth's Hospital in Washington D.C. to return from a long sojourn in private practice in Southern California to Atascadero State Hospital from 1990 through 1996, which is the subject of this study.

During his unique and varied career, Dr. Abrahams studied with, was in analysis and interacted with luminaries of American psychoanalysis such as Frieda Fromm Reichmann, Harry Stack Sullivan, James Rosen, Edith Weigert and Karl Menninger. He truly deserves a place, as this book demonstrates, as one of their peers. He has made singular contributions to psychoanalytic theory and practice, particularly with respect to the treatment of those patients who have been considered least accessible to traditional psychoanalytic therapy. Long before the seminal works of Kernberg and Kohut, which are referenced in the annotated bibliography, he developed successful models and techniques for treating patients with narcissistic and psychopathic personalities as well as psychosis and mood disorders.

Group therapy is a *sine qua non* for treatment of many of these individuals in which a Therapeutic Community develops, obviating the resistances, complications with dream analysis and thought disorganization which interfere with developing a stable working trans-ference relationship in individual therapy. The psychiatrist becomes a facilitator, who relinquishes the more authoritarian role assumed by the analyst in traditional psychoanalysis. As individuals progress they become amenable to individual work with analysis of the transference as the final project. Dr. Abrahams' group work has been successful with very large groups, families, mothers and daughters, professional identity groups, the severely regressed and psychopathic inpatients. This also includes his patients on two different wards and programs at Atascadero State Hospital. In both his group and individual therapy he has co-led with and trained various other therapeutic disciplines including pastoral counselors, which is consistent with diffusing and mitigating transfer-ence issues as well as getting at core "spiritual issues" as patients transact at the level of their souls.

His theories arise from his therapeutic experiences with patients, including self-analysis engendered by these transactions, as opposed to being formulated *a priori*. His "data" are encapsulated in extensive process notes with associated commentary. One important data source in his therapeutic work is what he characterizes as his "Intuitometer." This refers to physical sensations in his chest which he experiences during therapy and which confirm his deep emotional connection with the patient at a given point in the process.

Dr. Abrahams openly discusses how he arrived at various insights via iconic patients and his own dream analysis, therapeutic successes and failures. His deep and extensive reading in history, literature, the-ology, and psychoanalysis is reflected in his theoretical models. He is a Freudian analyst in the truest sense, understanding Freudian theory and practice at a level that he can use as a launching pad for his formula-tions, whose divergences he cogently explains. For example, he finds no support for Freud's Death Instinct theory, but Psychic Death, elaborated in the glossary, is a critical feature of his dynamic model. Messianism is a key concept in Dr. Abrahams' formulations, arising from universally recognized developmental conflicts and resolutions, reflected in Greek and other myths, such as the tale of Prometheus. Similarly, Psychic Death is exemplified in the complete version of the myth of Narcissus, which deals with pre-Oedipal issues.

Dr. Abrahams came to Atascadero State Hospital as a capstone to his career. During his long hiatus from inpatient work there had been significant changes in practice in institutional settings, particularly related to vastly larger psychotropic medications formularies, behavioral treatment protocols, especially for violent patients and sexual offenders. There additionally was a de-emphasis on psychodynamic and group oriented professional training and treatment, which now had an educational focus. His challenge was to see if his theories and practice were still relevant in an institutional setting, and if he could affect the kinds of institution-wide changes that had transformed St. Elizabeth's treatment milieu. In his judgment, his experiment was mostly successful for several overlapping reasons.

At the Ward and Program level, Dr. Abrahams' project was clearly successful. He initially shared a ward with another psychiatrist, who was an excellent psychopharmacologist. This mentor quickly brought him up to current practice with different classes of medications and how to use them synergistically. At the same time, Dr. Abrahams trained the other psychiatrist in depth psychological group work, by co-leading Therapeutic Community with him. Dr. German's perception of the benefits to himself and the ward are reflected in his encomium at the beginning of Chapter II. Dr. Abrahams had similar success on a subsequent ward with a different, more chronically institutionalized patient set. Other disciplines overcame their initial resistance and became actively involved in the group process as formulated and demonstrated by Dr. Abrahams.

At the institutional level the results were less satisfactory. There appeared to be two primary reasons for this. Both within the institution and mandated from the State, Atascadero was instituting programmatic change. Under a Treatment Improvement Project (TIP) initiated at the staff level a Psychosocial Rehabilitation model (PSR) was imposed, resulting in a major reorganization of the hospital. Before these changes could be finalized and fully processed by staff, the State Department of Mental Health instituted a Continuous Quality Improvement (CQI)) project, which further transformed the organizational functioning of the hospital. Notwithstanding these complications, Dr. Abrahams worked to integrate his Therapeutic Community model into the milieu. One of his tactics in this regard was embracing and becoming a leader in the PSR, then in the CQI process.

Ultimately, the institution, in spite of his efforts, began regressing and the Therapeutic Community project was not fully implemented. This tends to highlight one of Dr. Abrahams' theories of widespread group or institutional transformation. Change needs to be grassroots motivated and initiated. When it comes from the top down, in authoritarian fashion, as was the case with CQI, it tends to be rejected and/or superficially complied with. As he had noted with long-term patients, which applies equally with staff, they simply wait it out with the attitude, this too shall pass.

The other complicating factor, was that Dr. Abrahams, late in his tenure at Atascadero, was assaulted by a patient from another ward, who he did not have a treatment relationship with. He had noted the protective aspects for the therapist of having a patient in treatment. In this instance a patient from a unit with a strongly authoritarian regiment apparently displaced his anger with Dr. Abrahams as the object. Dr. Abrahams suffered a post-traumatic depression which did not respond to medication, but ultimately did resolve the abreaction in the analytic setting.

Two questions arise with respect to Dr. Abrahams' successful treatment with these patients using a psychodynamically informed group and individual treatment model. It is well known that psychotropic medications have cumulative benefits with patients who are commonly significantly better after a number of months compared with the first several weeks of treatment. One might assume that these hospitalized patients, virtually all of whom were on complex, sophisticated medications regimens, improved largely in response to their meds, and that psychotherapy was basically an adjunct that improved med compliance. This is belied by Dr. Abrahams' first ward assignment with a psychiatrist who was an excellent prescriber. The psychiatrist attested to demonstrable improvement in terms of court competency and other related behavioral and cognitive parameters.

Dr. Abrahams is a charismatic, uniquely talented and creative thinker and leader. He was able to maintain the delicate balance between the need for security, structure, leadership and focus in the group and individual setting, particularly in the high security institutional environment. At the same time he was able to foster a democratic approach of "mutual messianism" in which he and the patients transacted "man to man" in relative equality.

Volume I of this two-volume study provides Dr. Abrahams' perspective on these and other issues with respect to the institution as a whole. It also includes summaries of treatment in the context of key groups, Therapeutic Community and Living in Reality, and two individual cases with some case content and commentary, which exemplifies his approach. Included are summaries of his initiatives institution-wide, which replicate his prior work with family therapy, large group therapy and a psychoanalytic seminar. Volume II are the complete case notes with interpretation and commentary, which I found fascinating and revelatory. The critical transition between the two volumes are the

Glossary and Annotated Bibliography at the end of Volume II. They provide texture and context for the data and insights which follow.

Alienation is a key concept in Dr. Abrahams' formulation of mental disorders, and refers primarily to intrapsychic splitting or separation of the self. This can be manifested in rupture in relationships, regression to fixation at earlier developmental levels, and epiphenomena such as hallucinations, which can be understood as emergence into awareness of split introjects and associated affects. Dissociation or splitting of objects into all good or bad, as proposed by Kernberg can be aspects of alienation. Dr. Abrahams proposes that it may have an organic basis. This is consistent with the deep and persistent intrapsychic and behavioral manifestations. It may be demonstrable via PET, functional MRI or other technology, as has been the results of psychotherapy. Messianism and Psychic Death are two other important concepts.

In the more complete version of the Myth of Narcissus, the sage Tiresias predicted that he would die when he got to know himself. From a depth psychological standpoint, Narcissus' staring at his reflection suggests a mirror transference in which the maternal object lovingly reflects back to the infant in symbiotic union. When this bond is traumatically broken, Psychic Death can ensue. That threat of dissolution of one's identity leads to fealty to the worldview and assigned role in this internalized maternal object relationship. In successful therapy, as bonds to the internalized pathological object are loosened, patients typically experience depression, mourning and severe anxiety symptoms as they transition to living in here-and-now reality. Messianism is a broader concept, but plays a role in this drama in that one sacrifices aspects of oneself in fealty to the internalized "Godhead." Frequently, individuals who gravitate to the "healing" professions have a Messianic motivation, may have experienced a particularly close relationship with their mother and/or role reversal, in which they played a parenting role in their family. Regarding rebellious psychopaths, Dr. Abrahams notes that the messianic aspects of the transference imbues the therapist with the authority in the treatment relationship. The authority is earned as patients learn to trust the therapist as a constant, loving object.

Dr. Abrahams posits the Ego Ideal to play a much more central role in our psychological structure than in Freud's theory. This "Terra Incognita" of psychoanalysis provides the key to understanding our spiritual life and soul. It incorporates paternal introjects from the earliest developmental stages and determines our career(s) in life. The biblical Garden of Eden myth encompasses the loss of the idyllic maternal-self object fusion through a process of self-discovery, but in this case with a better outcome than Narcissus.

In the Annotated Bibliography, among many fascinating connections to Dr. Abrahams' theory and practice, August Aichhorn's group work with the antisocial stood out. "When not responded to in an authoritarian repressive manner, the antisocial leadership acted out powerfully, and at the height of hate and alienation they decompensate. . ." This was consistent with Dr. Abrahams' group work in which psychopathic personalities mourned as they let go of their alienated, transcendent position relative to group and became depressed or developed psychosomatic symptoms.

His section on Maxwell Jones, the forerunner of therapeutic community in group work, exemplifies the development of much of the theoretical and practical framework for Dr. Abrahams' approach with groups. Jones' decompensation late in his career also points to the risk in not continuing with self-analysis as an antidote to unanalyzed messianic impulses transmogrifying into grandiose delusions and a Bipolar diathesis.

In the group and individual case studies numerous concepts are explicated. For example, it is typical in groups for pro-social and antisocial leaders and cliques to emerge with the goals of collaborating with or undermining the therapeutic process. A "dialectic" ensues, which ultimately leads to a synthesis and furthering of treatment goals. In both individual and group therapy there are periods of progress alternating with regression, as patients retreat to a more autistic or psychopathic, less anxiety-provoking position. Over time mythic structures and internal object relations are clarified, dreams are more readily analyzable and the focus is on problem-solving in a here-and-now context.

The two individual cases whose detailed case notes are commentary comprise much of Volume II demonstrate the range and depth of psychopathology which Dr. Abrahams has addressed throughout his career. The first case is an individual with a chronic psychosis with hebephrenic features, who meets the criteria for Schizophrenia and has been institutionalized for many years. In many respects the early stages of his treatment are play therapy with the patient drawing on a chalk board stick figures or simple abstractions, exhibiting disorganized thought processes with here and now or past history admixed without clear demarcation with dream production. Dr. Abrahams synthesized and clarified central themes in the patient's productions, which over time lead to the patient's associations and dreams of becoming more organized and reality based. With respect to the aggressive behavior, that was not confronted or interpreted until Dr. Abrahams intuited an actual threat and said that they would have to decrease the frequency of visits if it continued.

The second individual case was with a long-institutionalized man with a severe personality disorder which was primarily psychopathic. His involvement in group therapy with Dr. Abrahams facilitated his eager participation in individual treatment. His dream production was voluminous. Numerous themes emerge around his ambivalently held maternal object relationship in which he was the special child, experienced role reversal, assigned responsibility for his several siblings, and was ultimately abandoned by her to foster care. He had a long history of cruelty to animals, who typically symbolize children. Over time through his therapy he experienced remorse along with the recognition of his displaced rage at his mother. There was similar progress with respect to his crime, rape, in commission of which he would enact various roles including controlling by bullying of his siblings. In parallel he became reconciled with his estranged family and abandoned his institutional prisoner identification for a prosocial one.

There developed a powerful maternal transference to Dr. Abrahams which came close to the patient's consciousness at times, but was not directly analyzed. This obverse of the patient's malignant identity was a messianic one along with a religiosity and anger at God and Jesus. Consistent with his practice and intuition Dr. Abrahams brought in Reverent Dodd as a co-therapist. Not only did that diffuse an intense transference, which was not ripe for analysis, but allowed the patient to develop a more realist, adult relationship with his God. Reverent Dodd readily embraced Dr. Abrahams' treatment style in that he interacted with the patient as an equal and was therapeutically self-revealing about how his own belief in the system evolved. They were truly a group of three.

Circles of Change is an apt title for my own history with Dr. Abrahams. I am a psycho-dynamically trained psychiatrist, who left private practice and started work at Atascadero State Hospital shortly before Dr. Abrahams in 1990. My career there lasted several years longer than his. We were friends and colleagues, but did not work directly together. In the year and a half prior to my leaving private practice I resumed analysis with my former training analyst, which facilitated my move. At this point I also considered resuming analytic training. One of my many regrets from that time at the State Hospital is that I did not take advantage of the training opportunities and the chance to work on institution-wide issues with Dr. Abrahams. I suspect that would have altered aspects of my subsequent career.

In retrospect, a "competitive messianic transference" such as Dr. Abrahams described with Maxwell Jones and his training analyst may have played a role in my resistance. Part of Atascadero's resurgence in the 1980s detailed by Dr. Abrahams in this study related to its "remedicalization" in which psychiatrists were, again, leaders of the treatment team. This attracted many of our well-trained and motivated colleagues to come there.

However, in what would have appeared a propitious environment for Dr. Abrahams and myself, significant obstacles arose. This included disruptive mandated programmatic changes, a non-psychiatrist as head of the State Department of Mental Health, an opportunistic, politically adroit organized psychologist created a recipe for institutional regression. In my own institutional career I followed Dr. Abrahams as Chair of the Psychiatry Department and then Chief of Medical Staff. I fought for the medical staff model and retaining the psychiatrist as the head of the treatment team, but was unsuccessful. Morale at the hospital suffered and the hospital became a more dangerous place to work.

Our paths diverged and we were not in contact for a number of years until the last year or so. We see each other regularly now and Dr. Abrahams graciously asked me to write the preface to this book. I can attest to the value of bibliotherapy and Dr. Abrahams as a uniquely gifted psychoanalyst with considerable patience, as this project has catalyzed my own self-analysis and taken far longer than either of us expected, but with results that for me have been very rewarding.

Our relationship has finally come full circle.

Barry Sugarman, M.D.
June 16th, 2016

Introduction

In this volume I shall assemble nascent thoughts and experiences traversed during my seven-decade career in the field of psychoanalysis with individuals and groups. More than that, I seek to test their validity in actual operation. The testing of hypotheses manifested itself in intrapsychic, personal, and social levels both in myself and the subject of my ministrations. Repeated success called for explanation and recognition of change in my self-concept. Conceptualization of the validity of these experiences brought about recognition of an advance in theory and practice. Thus was born, the epistemologic adventure of this book. In science, hypotheses are tested, but first generated. I came to the forensic institution Atascadero State Hospital replete with hypotheses concerning the nature of self and its change generated behind the couch, in consulting rooms, and meeting halls. They related to the larger issues of democratic self-governance on the part of the group and its correlate in the individual. In two volumes we become aware of the idealist birth of Atascadero State Hospital at the hands of its originator Dr. Reginald Rood. He attempted to meet the supreme challenge in modern psychiatry and penology of simultaneous furtherance of therapy and security. How that challenge was met is the subject of this book. There change was the order of the day in its circles of organization hospital wide and on my two Wards 10 and 24. I describe those circles of change for the general reader in Volume One and for the specialist in Volume Two. The reader is invited to participate in this adventure of understanding when the individual becomes alienated from self and others along with what enables reconciliation to occur.

CHAPTER I

Atascadero State Hospital Opens

The idea of an institution that sets about changing itself to achieve its self-governance, for the better is not new to history. At the national level we have the great revolutions—French, American, Russian and of course, the English. After throwing off autocracy, they set about changing their citizens toward liberation and self-development.

Philippe Pinel, the 18th century French psychiatrist whom some consider to be the father of modern psychiatry, broke the chains of the insane, and in doing so, the asylum movement was launched. But these liberating branches seemed to go astray and regress as has been history's course. The asylum movement started out affecting positive change, but then morphed into tyranny and baseness. In my study of history, I was especially interested in the role of leadership in the French Revolution, particularly to that of George Danton and Maximilien Robespierre. To my mind their failure and that of the incipient democratic institution led inevitability to regression and the Reign of Terror, then back to aristocracy. How and why the revolution consumed its originators became of central moment to me when I found myself in charge of the revolutionary development of therapeutic community. Mentally disordered offenders present one of the greatest challenges to changing themselves.

From the first, society has tended to alienate its offenders and mentally ill, seeking retribution from the former and isolation for the latter. John Howard, the 18th century philanthropist and prison reformer in England, pioneered prison reform in his country. This was followed in America by the establishment of state prisons. The word penitentiary stemmed from the act of penitence Quakers sought in the offender through spiritually based solitary confinement. In the United States, activist Dorothea Dix's work led, prior to the Civil War, to the establishment of asylums. In Dix's model, the asylum superintendent and his family lived at the facility amid a spirit of community. The psychiatrist was called an alienist, marking what I consider a central feature of both the mental and forensic disorder.

Atascadero State Hospital follows a similar course of progression and regression, of idealistic investment and disillusionment. The field of forensic treatment in its variable way had prepared the ground for Dr. Rood and his new hospital before 1954. Understanding this history is essential in order to make sense of its difficult course, through the tendency in forensic settings, more than most, to regress and enact the past.

Maximum Security and Prison Reform

In the period between the two world wars of the 20th Century, psychoanalyst August Aichhorn worked with delinquent youth in Vienna,

4

Austria. His book, *Wayward Youth*, enjoyed a wide circulation among educators. The book also mobilized the idealism of prison reformers, who were willing to experiment, then fall short, and in time, establish the building blocks of that most difficult of edifices, a maximum security mental hospital.

In the 1930s, a number of mental health professionals experimented with groups of patients, delinquents, and community members in ventures—correctional, educational, and psychiatric. S.R. Slavson, an engineer turned educator and therapist, was successful in developing programs for youth at the New York Jewish Board of Guardians. At St. Elizabeth's, Lazel conducted a psycho-educational group with schizophrenics, drawing them into the process of inquiry into their disorder. Professor Shaw's Chicago Area Project continues to this day, still dealing with delinquent youth by constructively engaging them in their community. In the 1940s, psychoanalyst Alexander Wolf's pre-war programs applied the Freudian method to group analysis of neurotics. Wolf went on to develop group treatment for delinquent soldiers during World War II at the Fort Knox Rehabilitation Center for Military Prisoners. Also during and after that war, Maxwell Jones pioneered in group treatment of war neurosis in England.

Alongside these ventures, there was a great deal of informal experimentation with ameliorative groups by the professions, as well as early initiative on the part of citizens afflicted with diseases such as alcoholism (Alcoholics Anonymous) and obesity. Early in my career as an Army psychiatrist, with nothing more than good intentions, I worked successfully in conducting a "class," with soldiers who suffered war neurosis.

It seems that the initiator of Atascadero State Hospital, Dr. Reginald S. Rood, exemplified the spirit and practice of the times, as well as the entrepreneurship he manifested in researching hospital architecture in America and Europe, then interfacing with California architects.

Rood envisioned a hospital which would function around the idea of group meetings to grapple with its problems in alienation. He devised a containment plan with an associated farm. California at that time was enlightened in its corrections and state hospital systems, and the hospital was built in 1954. The facility's Central Coast location, and the fact that the town of Atascadero had been planned as an ideal community, were undoubtedly influential in terms of where it was constructed.

Rood had previous experience with sexual psychopaths at Mendocino State Hospital, also in California, and was aware of a pilot study at Norwalk State Hospital near Los Angeles. His philosophy was "hate the sin, but love the sinner." He considered a model therapeutic experience for the psychopath to be 18 months in length, returning him to court with a "B" rating.

Rood also brought the patient-led discussion method, which was developed at Norwalk, to Atascadero. Psychologist Dr. Fred Cutter took it over when he joined the staff in 1955. Cutter met weekly with each leader and assistant leader, inferring their competency by their participation in his training group, and through his leadership modeling their behavior in their groups. Assistant Medical Director Thomas L. Gore developed a group psychotherapy program alongside the patient-led discussion groups. He required leadership of treatment groups by the professional staff.

Anthropologist Gregory Bateson served as a consultant at ASH from 1960 to 1963. He called for further attention to the mentally ill in the groups. Another contributor to the program was social worker Robert Ontell, who, most importantly, facilitated patient government.

Dr. Rood also sought active support of his experiment by the Atascadero city community by meeting with its residents, as well as having them visit the hospital. Rood established a working farm on the hospital's extensive grounds. In addition, wives and families of patients moved to Atascadero, which in time resulted in resistance on the part of the community because of the presence of child molesters and rapists.

As Atascadero State Hospital's first superintendent, Dr. Rood wrote a series of bulletins during his first four years that were distributed among staff and sometimes to the press. Following is a summary of those bulletins that will illustrate both his optimism and good will, as well as his naiveté.

Rood's Bulletins

July, 1954 to January, 1958
1954

Dr. Rood's first bulletin expresses gratitude for the work involved in the opening and dedication ceremonies. He commends staff and thanks the cadre of community volunteers for their cooperation and help. He announces the arrival of new patients from other hospitals and institutions, and names their diagnoses. In later bulletins that year, Rood announces the addition of yard security, as well as the development of new activity programs.

He finds the development of group spirit and departmental leadership to be notable. Rood warns against developing a prison-like character and admits the difficulty of applying the psychotherapeutic approach to the majority of patients, most of whom are child molesters and exhibitionists. He cautions staff that hostility toward and contempt for patients are incompatible with mental treatment. He advises personnel to approach a patient positively, because ". . . without treatment we are no longer a hospital; we have become a prison."

Rood reports that the hospital has a cooperative relationship with Department of Corrections that allows for the proper classification of incoming patients. He continues to announce new appointments as they arrive (nurses, doctors, therapists, supervisors and the like). He describes them all with the utmost positivity and continues to emphasize the hospital's patient centered focus.

Rood concludes the first years with a bulletin about the true meaning of Christmas and its reflection of the spiritual basis of our civilization, as well as truth and brotherhood.

1955

Rood's first announcement of the year is the inauguration of an advisory efficiency committee. He then discusses the availability of staff housing on campus, and announces additional transfers from Mendocino.

Rood reports that sexual psychopaths state they are happier at A.S.H. because they are treated more like human beings. He continually stresses accepting patients as persons, ". . . persons deserving of our hope and confidence." He also encourages joy, laughter, and smiling as being conducive to more effective therapists and patient outcomes.

A later bulletin announces the number of patients now eligible for probation through the courts, with release stats at 40 cases per month. The arrival of three new doctors is announced, including Dr. Fred Cutter as senior clinical psychologist. Again, Rood stresses condemning the act, not the person, in the same way that Christians are taught to condemn the sin, not the sinner.

In July of 1955, Rood marks the second year of operation. He announces that 200 sex offenders have been returned to society.

He then announces that an anonymous survey is being distributed among all staff, asking them to critique the administration and make suggestions for improvements.

By the end of the year, Rood announces that a total of 400 sexual psychopaths have been returned to the courts and probation, with only 5 of these violating probation so far.

1956

Dr. Rood begins the year by thanking his staff and lauding the success of stated treatment goals. He then announces the success of a program that encourages improving patients to help others improve as well. Rood quotes Bertrand Russell who warns against self-absorption as being a prison of its own making.

Rood reports an assault by a patient on a psych technician. He next warns against abusing patients, while stating that to date, none of his employees have been abusive and ". . . will not be, so long as we continue to respect patients as persons and fellow human beings."

In July, Rood announces plans for a family vacation, followed by a military leave as a major in the U.S. Army Medical Corps when he'll be stationed at the Fort Ord psychiatric section. More new staff are announced, with their credentials lauded, and a brief personal bio included.

1957

Dr. Rood reviews the first few years of operation, from July of 1954 to August of 1957. With a mission to provide effective therapy with security and safety, he states, "We have done excellently in this difficult assignment." He reports only 7 or 8% recidivism and the best safety record of all the hospitals in number of man days lost from injury. Rood reports an escape rate of 9 patients per every six months, stating that "recently," that rate was reduced to 4 per month. While encouraging stronger safety methods, Rood also states, "When security measures become too oppressive, we destroy morale and with it security. Success requires good judgment."

1958

Dr. Rood wishes one and all a Happy New Year, followed by a statement that interdepartmental good will is evident. He then quotes Tennyson, who said, "Cleave ever to the sunny side of doubt."

The Rood Bulletins conclude with the following noteworthy quote from Dr. Leslie Navran on the essence of the psychotherapeutic community. "All of therapeutic community program comes to this: if you treat patients as they are, they become worse. If you treat them as they are capable of becoming, they become better."

Without a research and development function to chronicle them, the data on what transpired in the groups are scarce. What is writ large in Atascadero State Hospital's history are the effects of escapees on acceptance by the community. Several months after inception, the hospital already had experienced patient escapes. The hospital reached its capacity of just above a thousand patients early in 1955. A year after inception, Dr. Rood touted the facility's uniqueness and success in lack of recidivism of its then-200 graduates. He praised ASH's security, citing that only one patient granted parole had walked off. Above all, he praised the community for its cooperation. But using a ladder, four patients escaped soon after.

Dr. Rood continued his effort at educating the public with an article in the *San Francisco Examiner*. In the article, as part of the program at ASH, Rood cited a basic fear of women as a motive for molestation, and social development of the patient though programmatic participation with women. It became apparent that the problem centered around issues in their self-governance and their inherent leadership. It was manifested in assault, escape, and finally murder. Seven patients escaped in mid-1960, and nine more inmates early the next year. That February, the Chief Deputy Director of the State Department of Mental Hygiene, in an investigation of the program and physical plant of the hospital, affirmed the validity of the program, its national significance, and the need for further security through remodeling and administrative measures. The following month, a patient with a record of previous murders killed an attendant.

It is important to state at this point that Dr. Brain, under whom I had worked some years before in the Veteran's Administration, asked me to head group therapy for the State of California. This developmental problem at ASH was one that I had encountered at St. Elisabeth's hospital, and had dealt with in accordance with the lessons I had learned at Fort Knox, which itself had used August Aichhorn's *Wayward Youth* as a model. There we had developed the model of therapy and security that Atascadero State Hospital in time sorely lacked. Central there was a training program, of comprehensive and intensive sort, for the personnel of all professions and grades.

In response to the murder of an attendant, a California state senator called for the removal of Dr. Rood. Dr. Blain, the Director of the Department of Mental Hygiene, took measures to improve security and the therapeutic program. Then a psychiatric technician was assaulted in a corridor, and Dr. Rood was called to Sacramento, the state capital of California, for a conference regarding the problems of security. Rood was then replaced temporarily by a Deputy Director of the Department of Mental Hygiene. Ms. Wiita, the Director of Nursing from the inception of the hospital, was replaced by Harold McAdam; Wiita was charged with irregularities in that process. The San Luis Obispo County Grand Jury adopted a wait and see stance.

In June of 1960, California Governor Edmund Brown addressed a forensic symposium that took place at Atascadero State Hospital. He spoke about the link between mental illness and crime, criticized the McNaughton "Right or Wrong" Rule, and affirmed the validity of the ASH treatment program. It is apparent to me that authority still was

11

motivated by hope and idealism, versus attending to the realities of a therapeutic community program. Judge David Bazelon took part in the event and later enunciated the Durham Rule, which placed Atascadero State Hospital at the center of liberalizing changes in criminal justice and its practice in treatment both of the "normal" and mentally disordered offenders in which substantial contribution to crime by mental disorder was acknowledged.

Then, in the fall of 1960, 11 inmates escaped from ASH by battering down a fire door. Dr. Miller leveled charges of security laxness, and refused to stand Officer of the Day duty, which resulted in a crisis situation. Dr. Rood was then transferred to Stockton State Hospital as Associate Superintendent, and was replaced by Dr. Louis Nash. Nash instituted changes regarding the control of keys, dining room cutlery, and movement of patients on the grounds. An interim superintendent, Dr. William Y. Hollingsworth, took the post for a short while, followed by Dr. G. Lee Sandritter early in 1961, who had transferred from Eastern State Hospital in Washington state. However, it turned out that Sandritter's hospital had problems similar to those at ASH, as well as "bush therapy," or illicit relations on the part of staff and patients. Sandritter had also been fired by the Washington governor. Some of his first changes were abolition of segregation by legal commitment, counseling of the patient by the same professional during his entire stay, and emphasis on a sense of community and socialization.

In 1962, ASH was accredited by the Joint Commission on Accreditation of Hospitals. The next year, Dr. Daniel Lieberman succeeded Dr. Daniel Blain in Sacramento, resigning after four months in office. Under Dr. Sandritter, ASH proceeded with an emphasis on group therapy. Sandritter resumed Rood's educational role with the press. In one interview, he emphasized the rehabilitative rather than punitive role of ASH, and the collaboration of patients in figuring themselves out.

The group therapy was starting to take hold, but insufficiently organized, escapes continued, and also in 1964, a patient who had been released four years earlier murdered again. This was followed in 1965 by another escape, this time by four patients, then another escape. Sandritter was replaced temporarily, then permanently, by the Associate Superintendent, Dr. Sterling Morgan. The hospital was reaccredited by JCHO in 1966, then suffered another patient death by stabbing, plus three by suicide in 1967. A low point was reached when three patients escaped by gunpoint, taking hostages in mid-1968. This was followed by a demand for tighter security by an employees union.

Dr. William M. O'Brien became Superintendent of ASH in mid-July 1971, serving briefly, to be succeeded on a rotating basis by other medical directors of other state hospitals, pending a nation-wide search for a new director. Alongside the search was scrutiny of ASH regarding changes to its programs, including medical record keeping, the performance of group therapy by doctors, and seclusion and isolation of especially dangerous patients. This rotation began with Dr. Freeman of Stockton State Hospital.

A sign of change was the appointment, in September of 1972, of a woman to the ASH security staff, in addition to the 63 women already employed in the security area of the hospital. A draft report of a review committee on charges of a task force on conditions at the hospital cleared staff of all allegations, centering on alteration of medical records.

Also later denied were rumors that ASH would be operating under the California Department of Corrections due to the phasing out of the state hospitals, and a change of jurisdiction from the Department of Mental Hygiene to the Department of Health. Governor Ronald Reagan's appointee to the post of Director of Mental Hygiene, William Mayer, announced that all hospitals for the mentally ill, except those in Napa and Camarillo, would be closed by 1977.

A.J. Rucci was made Medical Director of ASH in June, 1973, then Administrator in November of 1974. In March, 1974, a Citizens Commission for Human Rights toured ASH, and David Hamilton, Assistant to the Medical Director, stated that under reorganization in 1972 of the mental hospital system, the treatment approach of ASH was changed from psychiatric to non-psychiatric provision of care. Individual needs would be met under the new system.

A psychiatric technician training program was begun at Cuesta College, the area's local community college, in March of 1976. Behavioral psychologist Dr. Richard Laws announced a program for the behavioral treatment of Mentally Disordered Sexual Offenders, a treatment that encompassed exposure to evocative nude photographs followed by behavioral modification. Laws claimed that 54 percent of the inmates subjected to this technique made substantial progress. In 1977, ASH was sued for involuntary servitude and industrial peonage in its industrial program.

Later that year, an assault on four staffers brought about revelations of deficiencies in the alarm system, a reduction of staff from the 500 allocated to 300, and a complaint that only doctors could order behavior-controlling medication. Also that year, 340 signatures were gathered for a Letter of Grievance to be carried by Executive Director Sam Yockey to Sacramento. The letter centered around promotion and treatment programs. Two hundred persons protested in December, 1977, over the defective alarm system. Less than one year later, in November of 1978, overnight workers refused to report for work, claiming dangerous criminals were allowed to roam freely, their doors unlocked during sleeping hours. After five nights of this conflict, an agreement was reached over the role of evaluation in the locking of doors versus universal locking. Combat pay was also at issue.

Then, in July of 1979, a former sex offender and ASH patient Dr. Smith H. Washington shot and killed two Atascadero women.

Also that year, another former patient, Theodore Frank, was sentenced to death for the molestation and murder of a two-and-a-half year-old girl in Orange County, south of Los Angeles.

By February 1980, all medical and psychiatric vacancies were filled, and a comprehensive air conditioning system installed. In December 1980, Sidney Herndon, who had worked his way over a period of 21 years from psychiatric technician to executive director, assumed that post at ASH. In 1981, Karl Menninger lauded the program at ASH. A California State Assembly Criminal Justice Committee surveyed the Mentally Disordered Sexual Offenders program in March of 1981; its findings were critical of its application at ASH, especially the lack of psychiatric participation. The program ended in November of 1981, with future sex offenders slated to go to prison. Part of that agreement called for the treatment of mentally ill prisoners from the Department of Corrections.

In February 1983, the Civil Rights Division of the U.S. Department of Justice announced an investigation of inhumane environment and inappropriate use of seclusion and restraint. In January 1985, under the law abolishing the MDSO program, a new sex treatment program was initiated at ASH. The hospital girded for an influx of mentally ill prisoners by adding 35 new physicians, 20 psychologists, 35 social workers, 40 rehabilitation therapists, 100 registered nurses and 700 psychiatric technicians. Attacks on personnel were reported, then subsided.

After 30 years as ASH's medical director, Dr. Alfred Rucci retired in 1987, succeeded by Dr. Gordon Gritter. That year, the hospital was accredited by the Joint Commission on Accreditation of Hospitals, having lost its previous accreditation in 1976. Ground was broken for a child care center in October, 1987. Sidney Herndon was honored at a party in September of that year for ASH's accreditation. Still, the increase in assaults on staff resulted in a legislative move to add to an inmate's sentence.

Dr. Gordon Gritter then termed the new regimen "remedicalization." He reversed a regression to operational control by psychiatric technicians, and instead brought back the hegemony of the psychiatric department and the nursing staff. Gritter also rejuvenated the psychiatry department and its committee structure, with particular reference to its Patient Monitoring Committee and Psychopharmacology Committee. With the collaboration of Sidney Herndon and the growing array of disciplines at ASH, Gritter also furthered the development of clinical treatment teams on each of the hospital's 27 wards. Treatment there was led by a psychiatrist who coordinated the efforts of a social worker, psychologist, and rehabilitation therapist. A Director of Education, David Saunders, M.D., began to further the professional development of the psychiatric staff. Each unit was afforded offsite meetings for staff and unit. In collaboration with the other disciplines, Dr. Saunders mounted monthly multidisciplinary colloquia.

The crucial element of security rested in a collaboration with psychiatry, the nursing service, its psychiatric technicians, and the hospital security service. Psychiatry was in charge of medication management and, in collaboration with psychology, psychotherapy, which included therapeutic community. Nursing was in charge of the crucial emergency red light procedure, itself managed by a corps of psychiatric technicians, under initial intensive and continuous training. In addition, ASH's hospital security service policed the halls, periphery, and courtyards.

The therapeutic community regimen that was the centerpiece of the hospital, a program that Dr. Rood had instituted, had now fallen into disrepair, although it was still listed on each ward's standard procedures.

I could see my way clear to contributing to this great institution by adding my experience of four decades ago at St. Elizabeth's Hospital. Inevitable was a prospective engagement with the personnel in a training venture similar to that successfully enacted at St. Elizabeth's. This inevitably would have changed the relations of the professions to each other for the better. I joined the staff in 1990, and began an apprenticeship in a psychopharmacology that was of far greater substance than what I employed in my private practice.

Review of ASH's Course 1954 to 1990

One can discern in this troubled history periods of progression and regression, noted earlier in this volume for the proneness of forensic institutions to fall away from ideals of humaneness and progress. Dr. Rood strove mightily to combine the spiritual and secular in his profession of a revolutionary institution. It appears to me that he relied on collaboration by inspired fellow professionals to help organize the venture. Absent appeared to be systematic programmatic action such as that which came to ASH in the treatment improvement project that I first joined, then the state mandated Continuous Quality Improvement. Along the way the hospital floundered from crisis to crisis. A strong personality who had risen from the grassroots acquiring managerial expertise along the way, Mr. Herndon, turned the tide in the latter 1980s. He was joined by another strong administrator, Dr. Gordon Gritter, who brought the hospital back to higher medical standards. The medical psychiatric staff that Dr. Gritter assembled began initiative at a searching under the rubric of reorganization of the treatment process.

Atascadero State Hospital and the Quality Improvement Movement

During my years at ASH, there were extensive discussions to change its management style under the rubric of Continuous Quality Improvement. There was also an effort to work with families of patients on a comprehensive basis. Then, under my suggestion, a study group was formed, one that focused on the dynamics of the alienation of the patients, based on psychoanalytic writings.

Central to this work is the engagement of both the individual and his group toward changing himself. That is the premise of therapeutic community, an advance in treatment with wide social implications. That advance is consonant with the profound changes we are witnessing around the globe, changes brought about by the evolution of democracy and self-government from the grassroots, itself a revolutionary concept and practice.

Without such change, the best intentioned systemic changes can flounder. Writ large on the world's stage has been the last century's socialist experiment in Russia, with its ties to an authoritarian past best exemplified by Josef Stalin's Czarist character. Modern psychoanalysis has pioneered in exploration and resolution of those ties and that character, and beyond that, development of appropriate theory and practice.

Of equal importance is how we seek and report data, two elements that are central to the in-depth inquiry that is psychoanalysis. This book reports on my clinical experience at Atascadero State Hospital. It is written in narrative style, and features a running commentary that links the emergent data with past experience, as well as an inference on what ailed the members and their routes to recovery. The selves of the members were of principal focus, along with the phenomena of alienation and reconciliation. This focus involved reconciliation with self, one's natural groupings, and family.

Soon after the inception of this work, the hospital engaged in a massive administrative effort at self-change, which was mandated by the California Department of Mental Health. This change was modeled after the pioneering initiatives in industry, and elsewhere, of American W. Edwards Deming. The genius engineer, who was also a statistician, professor, author, lecturer and consultant, transformed Japan's postwar industry by using variants on his method. They were centered on what came to be called the Quality Circle, a formation for self-change analogous to that of group dynamics and therapeutic community.

Under the leadership of what was called its Quality Council, Atascadero State Hospital organized itself into a giant conference center, in which administrators and all the disciplines, down to the line personnel, engaged in systematic and highly structured working groups. Through preset modes of interpersonal exchange, these groups attempted determination of the managerial reality of what they were doing in accordance with the hospital's mission, always looking toward improvement of function. Issues that were addressed included safety, feeding of patients, movement through the halls and handling of patient records.

Since this endeavor took administrative precedence over what I had in mind in replicating training programs I had developed in group work, I joined forces with this effort in order to strengthen and deepen its group processes. I continued work on my assigned units in developing their therapeutic communities, as well as popularizing therapeutic community at ASH through colloquia. I also instituted a psychoanalytic seminar and a hospital-wide, family therapy program. Throughout, at its end, I kept in mind the research into regressive compulsivity and intuitive connectedness that I had commenced at the inception of my career.

This work is the fourth in a series centered on initiative of the individual and his group at self-change. The first book, *Democracy from the Grass Roots: A Guide to Creative Political Action*, addresses the grass-roots, the individual, and his reference group. Two others, *Turning Lives Around: Group Treatment of Military Prisoners*, and *This Way Out: A Narrative of Therapy of Sexual and Psychotic Offenders*, deal with forensic issues.

A fifth book, *An Adventure in Psychoanalysis*, was attempted after half a century of a psychoanalytic practice devoted largely to the severe disorders—obsessive, psychotic, and psychopathic—within and extra-institutional. There I had been able to extend the reach of psycho-analytic treatment to previously alienated individuals by utilizing a psychoanalytic approach which emphasizes intuitive connectivity.

This connectivity came as a surprise to me. Indeed, it was at the inception of my career as a psychiatrist, and before formal training. During World War II, I was in charge of an experimental group therapy for young Army offenders. The members, usually raucous and disruptive, grew silent and contemplative, then cooperative. This became systematic, inducing deeper study. We discovered this: my staff and I had experienced a poignant sensation in our chests during the silences. The result was a formulation of hypotheses about intuitive connectedness, as well as the presence and awareness of what came to be called an intuitometer. The intuitometric phenomenon plays a prominent role in this study, and is featured in its running commentary.

The data of this report stems from written notes of each encounter, therapeutic and otherwise, deemed relevant to the development of therapy at Atascadero State Hospital. My model for the daily notes stemmed from previous research methodology that was developed in conjunction with Jerome Frank and Florence Powdermaker, reported in the volume, *Group Therapy* (Harvard Press, 1953).

What I was trying to do at ASH was replication and extension of what became increasingly sophisticated treatment programs, which began with the afore-mentioned Fort Knox Treatment Program for Military Prisoners, then the program at St. Elizabeth's Hospital in Washington, D.C., as well as Hanbleceya, a private institution for the treatment of young schizophrenics in San Diego, California. All are described in detail in the bibliography.

Family Therapy at Atascadero State Hospital

Although untrained in psychiatry, ASH executive director Dr. Reginald S. Rood, from the beginning of his tenure, instituted a family spirit among staff and patients. This philosophy was exemplified by his systematic letters to the staff. In this spirit, members of the staff conducted family relevant groups. In one of them, a psychologist met with a group composed of patients and their wives. These spouses had relocated as families to Atascadero in order to facilitate weekly meetings with their husbands. All went well until antagonism toward the hospital on the part of its neighbors resulted in termination of the program by Dr. Rood.

Some years later, a psychologist and psychiatrist instituted a ward composed of patients who had maintained contact with their family members, and in which they met monthly on what we called Family Day. This was terminated because of objections by personnel of a security nature. I, too, tried to institute systematic family therapy on a hospital-wide basis during my tenure at Atascadero State Hospital. Those efforts are reported in the chapter on family therapy, terminated as such in favor of an educational model.

This outcome, short of the goals of therapeutic community, is illustrative of the difficulty I experienced in the intervention at ASH.

The title of this book, *Circles of Change: An Adventure in Therapeutic Community at Atascadero State Hospital*, could easily deceive the reader into thinking that ASH was transformed as were St. E's, the Fort Knox Rehab center, and the Über Hollabrunn of August Aichhorn. We fell short at ASH, and that's part of the adventure. On the following pages are detailed the vision, hopes, and denouement of that effort.

CHAPTER II

Therapeutic Communities at ASH

Introduction by Michael German, M.D., Chief Psychiatrist

The word psychotherapy comes from two ancient Greek words: psyche, meaning soul and *therapeia*, denoting cure. Reaching to the patients' souls was the cornerstone of Dr. Abrahams' treatment. I was privileged to work on the same unit with Dr. Abrahams. There, he was my mentor, group leader and role model. The unit is discussed elsewhere in the book, but let me touch upon some core aspects.

When Dr. Abrahams came to the neurobehavioral unit, group therapy as such was non-existent. The meetings we had were informational. Controversial items were not discussed in detail and if they were mentioned, it was in passing. There was a pressing need for a format where the patients would present their feelings and issues and work on their resolution.

When Dr. Abrahams presented his ideas regarding group therapy, he was met with resistance from the patients and the staff, each for their own reasons. The former did not care and wanted to be left alone. The latter were concerned that bringing troubling matters out in the open could lead to more acting out behavior, instability, and assaults. Only the energy, devotion, perseverance and highest professionalism on the part of Dr. Abrahams led to concrete results.

They say that every beginning is difficult. That proved to be true. However, the milieu slowly learned to adapt to the new ways. The staff accepted that group therapy was here to stay. It was won over when it saw that conducting regular groups was productive and led to more stability on the unit. There were fewer red lights and fewer assaults. The most rewarding factor was that the patients participated willingly and openly. Of particular interest was the fact that the patients here were not the run of the mill. Many had neurological cognitive deficits along with mental disabilities. The fact that they worked cohesively and were able to tackle ward problems as well as their own deserves special praise.

The attrition rate was low and mostly caused by transfer, discharge, or appearance in court. Their stability led to more successful competency training.

This chapter contains a lot of factual material, transcripts of some of the sessions, each subjected to thoughtful analysis. It is well written and would be of interest to the experienced psychotherapist as well as the beginner. Reading it was a relived experience for me. All the patients in the group and the staff suddenly sprang to life. Each session was like a mini-drama, with its conflicts, convoluted relationships, and happy endings. The book evoked in me a deep nostalgia. In my memory, Dr. Abrahams appears like a bright light, a shining star that cannot be replicated.

Therapeutic Community on Ward 10: A Schematic Summary

Each unit in the hospital was enjoined, through inclusion in the standard ward procedures, to mount a daily or less frequent meeting of its patient population, plus appropriate staff, to deal with administrative and therapeutic concerns. That procedure stemmed from the hospital's beginnings, described in the historical account in this volume. Yet at the time of this work, only three units abided by this mandate. One on Unit 28 was centered on inclusion of the families of the patients, with periodic "family days;" the other two met one to three times weekly to deal systematically with ward issues and to socialize the patients. I had in mind a fuller psychotherapeutic experience, stemming from my previous work in Howard Hall and elsewhere.

After assignment to Unit 10, I conferred with my team members, consisting of the unit psychiatrist, the ward nurse, a social worker, a rehabilitation therapist, and a psychologist. All were enthusiastic about starting therapeutic community meetings, except for the nurse, who expressed concern about loosening of control on the part of the patients and marring a newly waxed floor. In the face of this resistance, which I sensed was deep seated, I demurred, but the rehabilitation therapist forged ahead, and we began.

The success of therapeutic community on Ward 10 can be attributed to continuation and replication of a special experience I had gone through in World War II. There, at the Fort Knox Rehabilitation Center for Military Prisoners, the task was also part educational, part character transformation, and part recovery from mental illness. In the midst of the emergency of preparation for combat, we mounted a well-rounded program. We ran a remedial school in reading and writing. We held classes on motivation to fight the war. We taught combat skills. But above all, we emphasized the task of living in this new and dangerous reality. This had a psychoanalytic basis and background introduced to this account in Chapter I: Atascadero State Hospital Opens.

Only 40% of the rehabilitees were deemed suitable for insertion into the ranks for the Battle of the Bulge that was then raging. 70% of our graduates were successful. We learned the necessity of close-in leadership throughout the process.

Analogous to the task of the wartime Fort Knox Rehabilitation Center to restore rehabilitees to combat, Ward 10's task at ASH was limited to resumption of the ability to appear in Court, to comprehend the charges against one, the roles and responsibilities of the court officials, and to conduct one's defense in a relatively realistic manner. The patients on Ward 10 needed a certain amount of forensic schooling, treatment for their mental illness, resocialization, and much more individual attention than did the rehabilitees at Fort Knox. Such attention is characterized later in the literature as therapeutic alliance.

The therapeutic community meetings were led basically by the treatment team. In my previous work in therapeutic community, I solely conducted the sessions, followed by an *ad hoc* conference of visitors and personnel. This was a decade before development of the team approach. Now, though I was ostensibly in overall charge of the group sessions, the team members had their spheres of function, and were asked to join in guiding its progress. I had the option of taking over to bring the process back on course.

It is vitally important to note that security considerations called for readiness to switch from the nurtured, emergent democracy of therapeutic community to a previous authoritarian approach, with its hierarchy. The boss would take over and restore order and safety. However, as the sessions proceeded, and the powerful dynamic of the group became evident, personnel and patients willingly deferred to my prior experience, and the new way of therapeutic community.

When I first joined the unit, the reality was that I needed acculturation. I had long experience in a maximum security institution, Howard Hall at St. Elizabeth's, and had dealt successfully with consummately violent people, but that was 40 or more years ago. During those years, I had been safely ensconced behind the couch in a psychoanalytic private practice. Would the personnel and patients have confidence in this newcomer psychoanalyst's judgment and sureness of decision in moments of crisis?

I was now serving an apprenticeship, where the ward psychiatrist was my proctor in medication management. He supported the idea of starting the Therapeutic Community. As I have noted, the charge nurse and the psychiatric technician who supervised the personnel who controlled the patients opposed its inception. His psychiatric technicians would be the ones injured. The charge nurse was vocally against it because the patients would be agitating one another, getting out of control. In addition, the dedicated housekeeper had put so much effort into waxing and polishing the floor! I noted to myself that I had gone through a similar transitional conflict 40 years previously in the maximum security section of St. Elizabeth's Hospital, vividly reported in my volume *This Way Out*.

The need for a stable order was made imperative by the special mission of this ward: preparation of its members to stand trial on return to court. They were clearly unsuitable for trial, still too unstable or regressed, given to berserk violence, disorganized speech, and self-seclusion. The treatment would be part reversion to classroom, part structured life style, but mostly emotional re-engagement in which the subjects would be motivated to face justice. Therapeutic community, with its inherent motivational dynamic, was most suited to that end. Learning followed re-rooting in reality.

The ward community—patients and personnel—were expected to attend, and were theoretically responsible and answerable to one another. In addition, the group was theoretically self-governing, holding its members to account. Its subgroups, in an ongoing workshop format, would report their purview and findings. The group agenda followed this template, with initial orientation to the calendar day, the schedule of meetings, reports of the officers of the ward such as sergeant at arms, patient government chair, etc. Then came the trivial pursuit game, followed by the general discussion period led by a professional. On some units, the entire process was led by patients, under the guidance of the professional staff.

Staff had conflicting views on proper procedure, mostly along the lines of an educational intervention called behavioral modification, in which the template was determined by personnel aiming to win the patients over to their vision regarding attitude and behavior. This was versus the more grassroots, psychoanalytic approach of group psychoanalysis, in which the roots of awareness and motivation stemmed from the patients, in engagement in therapeutic alliance with the personnel.

As noted, this was illustrated at the inception of this therapeutic community by a conflict with the ward nurse, who opposed the initial meeting of the ward group because the newly waxed floor would be marred, and this would discourage the housekeeper. Ostensibly, her efforts were to inspire the patients to again love neatness and reality. The treatment team differed, and went ahead, resulting in a state of partial alienation on the part of the ward nurse and chief psychiatric technician, which was eventually resolved, coincident with the evident strength of the therapeutic community in motivating and controlling its members. Achieving the theoretic democracy of pure therapeutic community underlay all, falling short, but with the consent and participation of the entire community, was led ultimately by the personnel.

The team was in charge of therapy, and the charge nurse and psychiatric technicians in charge of security. Their disagreement over the inception of therapeutic community only heightened the danger. The team members, consisting of the two psychiatrists, psychologist, social worker, and rehabilitation therapist, had quickly arrived at the issue of the roles of the members. The rehabilitation therapist was experienced in dramatics and patient self-government, and would be the initial leader. She favored forming the patients into concentric circles. Recognizing her capacity to lead, I agreed. This left the nurse and psychiatric technicians incipiently alienated, as noted. My analytically oriented work would be done in the context of an operant, self-governing group seeking to enact reality in its way of governing itself.

The Sessions Begin

Before launching into the story of the transformation of an extremely antisocial and asocial population into a group which constructively worked on its problems, I would like to render the reader some further background data. It is important to note that of the twenty eight living units at Atascadero State Hospital, a total of three assembled the patients to engage in constructive activity of the sort designated as therapeutic community. In one the attempt was to socialize them so that they behaved agreeably with one another. Another brought them together with their families systematically for socialization and study by the personal. A third used the group formation to indoctrinate the individual with prosocial values. I early recognized these approaches to be of value, but they did not result in the basic change that I had noted earlier in my wartime experience at Fort Knox. This crucial change occurred at its inception in the form of a revolutionary abandonment by psychopathic, delinquent offenders of their alienated positions in favor of collaboration with their therapists toward reconciliation with self and society. Thereafter as a mission I sought nothing less than this as my therapeutic goal. Such was my aim in starting the ward group on unit ten.

The story of ward ten starts with my apprenticeship in the ways of a maximum security rehabilitative facility, which centered on administration of potent medication as the chief instrument of recovery for its problem patients.

It is of importance to describe and characterize the population of this ward, numbering twenty-four. All had severe difficulties living in reality sufficient to rendering them incapable of appearing in court for adjudication. Several were floridly psychotic, living in other worlds. A number were obsessed with the imperative to assault without apparent provocation. Many lived in interior worlds, refusing to attend to their self-care or acknowledge the existence of others. Several enjoyed deceiving the other, whether fellow patients or personnel. The therapeutic task was preceded by the need for safety and structure. Medication for psychosis, hyperactivity, and alteration of mood were employed systematically.

The centrality of maintenance of order and its attendant safety were shown in the high value that the chief nurse and unit supervisor placed on housekeeping details. Central there was maintenance of a clean waxed floor in the common area.

On the basis of my account of previous experience with therapeutic community, my treatment team and I had arrived at an enthusiastic stance of starting one on this unit. The rehabilitation therapist of the team volunteered to be the moderator. We consulted with the charge nurse on the matter, who promptly demurred, on the basis of the freshly waxed floor, which would be marred by footprints and dragged furniture. Respecting the need for caution, I delayed the venture. However, the rehabilitation therapist audaciously announced the first meeting of the group in a day room. She had also taken the trouble to assemble chairs in a circle in the middle of the room. I moved to join the several patients who had watched her closely, as did the ward psychiatrist and the unit psychologist. All of us were expectant of either success or deep conflict with the charge nurse and her associate, the unit supervisor.

One of the members, Jones, who had been ever ready to assault his fellows or the personnel, started things off by shouting that he did not want to attend. Others began seating themselves, and the rehabilitation therapist began the proceedings with the game of Trivial Pursuit. By this time twelve members had joined. The rehabilitation therapist then called on me to speak. I noted that the circle represented something more than a circle: it was a way of showing what we were about, facing reality and one another, man to man. Jones stated he was made uncomfortable facing people and reality. I asked if he wanted to. He stated with a smile that he didn't, that he would like to go back to our old way. He followed that by stating he didn't like that way either. Another member joined in. Jones then stated he voted to have it the old way. On the basis of previous experience, I took him to be yielding to current reality sufficient to change from the "dog-eat-dog" prison gang enforcement he would have employed otherwise. He was yielding to the democratic mode of decision by vote.

The next session was even more dramatic in relation to the potentiality to violence. The chief protagonist there was Darrow who, on leaving the safety of outer space in his mind, became instantaneously prone to violence. He got up from his chair and leaped to center stage in the middle of the group in a fighting manner, ending it in a mode where he mimicked Jackie Gleason, a prominent television comic who finished his song and dance with a characteristic, "Away we go!" Had he continued with the wild gesticulation, I or the ward psychiatrist would have called for initiation of the procedure called red light, in which close to a dozen psychiatric technicians from this and other wards would have assembled to take Darrow in hand. Instead, I was gratified that he ended his exhibition in a jocular fashion. Safely within our reality, he denied stealing cigarettes. During his gesticulation other patients mocked him as crazy, then eventually subsided. The ward psychiatrist had turned to me on addressing the issue of a red alert. A nurse stated her surprise at how well Darrow took the mocking by his fellow patients. Darrow continued protesting his innocence, sat and rejoined the body of the group. The rehab therapist then congratulated the group on how they had handled themselves, ending the session. In his mind, Darrow had been living in outer space, punctuated on earth by massively violent outbursts. Here he is moving from a psychotic identity to a less alienated one. A nurse had that background in mind when she congratulated him for containing his anger. My hypothesis is that here he returned to earth in identification with a television star. He certainly appeared coherent and grounded in the post-session interview. The nurse and the rehab therapist, in their display of cognizance to the interior life of this problem patient, had made a contribution to the advancement of the group as a therapeutic instrument.

Under the thesis that the devil is in the details, we shall go through the next sessions step by step. They occurred a month after the session cited above, a month in which there was steady gain in the capacity of the group to stick to the point and accept working together. I provided linkage to the previous session in which Moran had professed fear of return to his escape of reality by drinking. By this time Jones had turned to becoming a prosocial leader in the group, and suggested to Moran that he should attend the Alcoholic Anonymous. Moreover, he volunteered to bring me to a meeting of ASH's AA group. Moran allowed as how he might be willing to do so. I noted that Snodgrass had been volunteering to help Moran get his act together for his prospective meeting with the team. Jones noted that Snodgrass had been in room seclusion for a while, for having his pants down. The members then sought to instruct me in the prison code as they experienced it lately. By this time, the ward had started looking forward to the therapeutic community session and all patients and ward personnel attended voluntarily. The social worker led this session, which was brief because of time constraints. He asked the members where the previous group was at its ending. There was a long silence and I decided to fill in for the members by furnishing data on model behavior. Sensing that their resistance had to do with snitching, I then decided to model that behavior. A member stated definitively that were children raised "properly," there would be no addiction. I was delighted with this prosocial stance. It also appeared to me that the group was entering into dynamics similar to that of an AA group, where the members shared their problematic behavior in good faith on the way towards coming to grips with an alteration of their problematic selves. Of note was the participation by personnel like Karen in the discussion. I had sensed that the group was moving towards conceiving of their problems as deviant characters. The members began evidencing awareness of Jones's authoritarian character and his need to alter it for acceptance. At the same time, the group and I became aware of our emotional ties and of missing one another's presences. Jones joined the group at the end and announced, standing up, that he was going to "take Snodgrass and punch his face" for farting in his face in the toilet that morning. He also demanded his hall card back; he claimed he had worked six weeks hard to get it up to level III. Snodgrass and Glasure cited Jones's bullying ways. Farrell stated that his own behavior resulted in the suspension, and that it had started earlier, with his pushing Castellanos around, about sitting on the sofa. The ward psychologist brought up that Jones had employed racial slurs, which was inappropriate. Jones grew more heated and threatening. The rehabilitation therapist and I moderated during these interchanges, and invited Jones to rejoin the circle. He did so. The intensity calmed down. The discussion then moved to Jones' horse play in the morning, which the group, except for Hurd, found disruptive. It was 8:50 by this time and time was up. I noted I was going to visit Adams on Ward 20. After noting I had heard he missed the group, I asked whether members missed him. Smith, Hurd, Snodgrass, Glasure and others stated they liked him and missed him, and wanted me to convey that to him. Snodgrass later brought Adams' cup, for me to take to him. Jones appears drawn to becoming centerpiece, subject of discussion of his domineering and passivity. He demonstrated the latter, *en passant*, when he yielded to us about rejoining the group. That reconciliatory event was exemplified regarding the members' heartfelt sentiments concerning an absent member of the group. The next session is reported in detail because of its transitional nature, towards a self-propelled therapeutic community, operating with me and alongside of me on its own.

Darrow Helps Ahmed; Beginning Discussion of Paranoid Delusions

Ahmed resisted going to the group, remaining off to the side. He then yielded. Jones complained about dust from the air conditioning system, and was joined by Snodgrass. They alleged that there was a thick pile of dust under the vents. The rehabilitation therapist stated for them to type it out and hand it in; "have your representative come here." I asked

Smith about an ASH Community Council member attending one of our sessions. Smith stated he was to come on Thursday. Next, I brought up two items for the agenda with the caveat that there was not enough time. Ahmed then brought up he had lost his glasses. Darrow stated he had seen the glasses and the case on a gurney two days ago. Rossi broke in regarding the dust, and went on that there was "electricity coming from the walls."

Angel then opened up, laughing and gesticulating. I asked him what he was talking about. He stated he was afraid of being jumped, and wanted to be like a character from the movies. The ward psychologist stated that the character was a hero who was out to win against great odds. Angel agreed. I stated that he wanted to be strong and manly. He added "So people won't make fun of me and jump me." We had run over our time.

After the session ended, Marshal asked to speak briefly to me and began complaining of the guff people gave him about his uncivilized way of eating and his reciprocal criticism of theirs. He stated he wanted to join the Army. Angel came over to state he had a way of partying when he was younger, and, at my instance, that he wanted to clean up his act. He then stated his fear of assault for his way of laughing at people.

I noted it as more than coincidence that they had joined me for post therapeutic community session talk on eating and motivations thereon.

Commentary

Microanalysis of this session would reveal at least three cycles of self-revelation on the part of the members, each more into reality and life course issues and reports. An example of increased existence in reality

was Darrow's here on earth report of the location of Ahmed's glasses. The cycles culminated in Angel's report of his hedonic excess in his youth, its reflection on his character, and his desire to come into reality, with suggestive hebephrenic laughter that in my past experience edged towards tears.

In the next two sessions, the members gave evidence of an interest in communicating their problems with themselves and others, also of their connection with one another.

The next session is cited again in some detail, evidencing significant movement toward attainment of therapeutic community.

Ruiz and Marshal Reveal Underlying Sadness Regarding their Life Courses

This session began at 8:15 am. A nurse and psychiatric technicians were present, a matter of seminal significance. It was begun by the rehabilitation therapist with Trivial Pursuit cards. The members entered into it moderately well, with some criticism about the cards as out of date. Then followed announcements concerning clinic appointments and doctors' calls. The group discussion proper started at 8:25. Members asked me how my cataract eye surgery went. I noted it went well. They asked if I saw better. I answered them in simply human terms that it would take a few days for my tissues to settle down. I then asked what happened yesterday. The social worker reported that the group helped Marshal with his legal difficulties. Many patients talked at length with him to help him straighten things out, and he received a lot of support. I noted that I had talked with him, and was gratified that he was able to get to the point better now. Then Prince got up and said he was going to cruise, wouldn't listen to this. I noted that as an escape from reality, from talking it through.

Then I brought up the problem of Ruiz and his loss of cigarettes and food he had purchased at the canteen. Part of it he had given to others, but most someone had stolen from his room. A nurse stated that visiting in rooms would most likely be restricted. She then added that if the cigarettes would be returned, no questions would be asked.

The group went further into the situation of Ruiz and his loss, with a half-dozen members stating that most would want to steal from others, but that Ruiz had given his cigarettes away. Ruiz stated that members were lying when they claimed he gave away so much, that it had been stolen. I noted that prison psychology had it that you gave when you had, and got when you needed it, which was all right, but that called for somebody who could take care of himself, not give the shirt off his back when you did so. They would take the undershirt, too!

I turned to Ruiz and noted that he had asked for help with becoming a real man, that formerly his hope was the Army, and now he was letting the group talk these things through with him. I asked his permission to mention something he had brought up in our talk that day. He consented. I noticed he used Marshal as a model of somebody who got somewhere in his life; "I have my doubts about the man, but he did make something of his life." Ruiz agreed. Someone mentioned that Ruiz needed a conservator. I noted that the group was enacting that role at the moment.

Time was up, and I summarized to the effect that the group had talked helpfully with two members, one with considerable intellectual power, with a good head, and the other who acts like he doesn't have one, helping both. We ended on a positive note. Afterwards, Marshal encountered me about his plan to get an attorney he had contacted first through the VA, which I doubted as a likely option, then through his friends. I offered to talk with his attorney about straightening it out. He stated that the lawyer was in it for the money and in league with the judge, whom he would sue. Then he noted his offense itself for the first time with some emotion, which he communicated to me. He agreed that the emotion was present. I noted the impression that he had a strong sense of identity and integrity, and that he was mortified by being in such a position. I experienced sadness from him, noting that he could cry. He replied that he doesn't cry. We then had to stop.

Commentary

I am positing that there is a connection between Ruiz' poignant helplessness and that of Marshal, who is on the verge of revealing emotion concerning his crime.

This next session is illustrative of the regression and progression inherent in therapeutic community with the severely disordered.

Self-Revelation and Intuitive Connection

Four months after inception, Moran unburdened himself about his low estate in life, and his transcendence of depression through autistic fantasy. Darrow at times relinquished reality in outer space for assertion of one on earth. Jones and Rossi led the members in a group revolt of abstinence from attendance, while intuitively connected. One member edged towards revelation of his paranoia, experiencing electricity coming from the wall.

I noted to the members next my feeling that I had not said a proper goodbye to several members who had just left, and made the observation that they had improved greatly from their regressed states on hospitalization. The members agreed. They progressed further in the next session, arriving at a wish to extend the program to encompass more activities. The members worked then on Myles' violent outburst in the patient's dining room, which was self-emulative, and the helpful nature of full bed restraints in settling one down.

The members gainfully inquired into a violent altercation that took place between Horvathton and Darrow over the rights to a borrowed cigarette. This again led to Darrow's assertion of his sense of reality. He defended his role in settling space wars, while advocating the development of perspective in viewing the vast universe. His exposition led Loring, alienated from his mother, to broach renegotiating their relationship. That led Smith to assert how his family is coming together, and Marshal was moved to bring up his alienation from his twin daughters.

Then, six months after inception of the group, there was a seminal session, in which Moran engaged in hypomanic verbosity, dominating the scene and leading to consultation among the members on what to do. Darrow was prominent there, soberly advising me to use a combination of medication and dialog. In the next session, I essayed an interpretation that involved regression to a deathlike agony, combined with alienation from himself. Then, in a following session, I checked Moran's obstreperous behavior, which he accepted, eliciting the datum from Loring on his need for a father's hand, which Moran extended.

A member stated he felt empty inside when the doctor was gone for the weekend. The members collaborated in support of Marshal, who reported he "gave up the ghost" in regards to his sense of weirdness. Then the members entered into a long negotiation regarding a tobacco pool, centering on the issue of trust. Prince, who usually spoke only to state that time was up, joined in discussions. The group had been established as a central factor in the lives of the patients. The issue of thievery was exemplified by Moran in his invasive behavior with his fellows, parallel to that in his crime.

Jones qualified to return to court, and was acknowledged by the members and doctor for his contribution. Despite his being the leader of a tentative antisocial gang, he had volunteered for the position of timekeeper, which was taken over later by Prince. The members engaged in a long silence about the tobacco pool, finally deciding not to have one. The rehabilitation therapist left for the post of Director of the Patient's Canteen, with testimonials from patients and personnel.

Accepting the Therapeutic Community

The chief nurse and unit supervisor, who had originally opposed its inception, visited the group and now officially acknowledged its usefulness. In doing so, they were deviating from the hospital's repressive mode of keeping order and safety. The unit supervisor noted the ease of communication. He had previously found it to be like pulling hen's teeth. Loring became poignant about his alienation, and Darrow waxed eloquent about his life in outer space, on the way to quitting it. The members were working into analysis of the aggressive, authoritarian aspect of their characters, as well as the rebellious, psychopathic side. This was demonstrated in the Snodgrass-Myles conflict. Snodgrass is pointing out, by not being afraid of it, Myles' authoritarianism, which he, Snodgrass, is persecuting by bumping him. He was bullying the bully, mutely. His ire, in which he wanted to beat him unconscious, appears to stem from his personal history. Members, especially Moran, were leaving their autism to be helpful messianically. We were on the verge of reaching into these arenas analytically.

For several weeks the group considered establishment and maintenance of a tobacco pool based on an honor system, discussing its administrative challenges. This evoked responsible behavior on the part of patients like Snodgrass, who was a member of Jones' gang previously. Prince's graduation assured a ritualistic turn, with inquiry into the impatient, authoritarian character that underlay his masochistic rebelliousness. He participated in the group, but only by calling it to an end as timekeeper.

I found myself able to coordinate contending factors in the group, such as Snodgrass, and White joined me in that endeavor. Then Snodgrass came out with the statement that there were two sides to every argument. I reported that I was touched by his emotion. The members brought up the devil's influence and their impulses to touch sexually, all messianically related. Hilton admitted possession by the Devil. This was a pivotal point in the development of the group.

The theme of devil possession was personalized by Marshal, in which he and the members went ambivalently into his crime of arson, in which he burned his trailer for vengeance. Members encouraged him to take the test for preparation for trial, the CAT test, in which he took his paranoid self in hand, braving what he anticipated was a biased judge. Members applauded.

With Loring as point man, the members then edged into the issue of a productive life. Loring began it by attacking me for not doing anything with his CAT test. The members reflected to him his passivity in that regard. Mosha's self-punishment and Gallenger's beleaguering Baggett for slowness were next taken up by the members in a positive manner. Waleed then emerged from an agonized state that I elicited and had to do with feeling abandoned by his girlfriend. Our togetherness in the rehabilitation group was discussed.

It became increasingly apparent that Mosha, Waleed, and Loring exemplified hatred of self for failings, and Moran and Marshal were at nadir, for failing in their life endeavors. The members accepted my interpretation to that effect. We agreed that we enjoyed trivia, and I stated that one did not know where the next answer was coming from, a manifestation of the members' increasing cognitive capacity.

The members have arrived at the point where they join with me in emotionally holding a representative age-regressed member, identifying with him and bringing up life course issues that they understand first-hand. It is of note that I have been participating with a number of them in a sing-along, also dancing with Waleed in what I sensed was a simply human manner. Loring and Waleed are particularly boyish, representative of the members, who are edging into the transaction, in this instance about negativity. The session was marked by advances in the group's capacity for free association, intra-psychically and interpersonally; also by amplification and exemplification of previous content.

We have advanced in the discussion, bringing in members representative of reality-based material, as well as inherent mythic self-concepts. Most important, we touched on the affective elements: loss, death, and anger. Alonzo took another step at reintegration of his personality and dealing with the transferential elements—relation with a mother figure, and also at one point, the instant offense. He was accused of raping an older woman. My thesis is that through therapy and the loss of his psychotic omnipotence, he is regressing. He had also lost his father through death, his original nuclear family through divorce. Regarding his inability to deal with his depression, he had stated he was not able to cry when his father died. A characterological fixated identification with his father had left him crippled, as well as still inside the undetermined symbiosis with his mother.

An "Impossible Patient"

The patient Calendar was drawn into the group dynamic at the point of identification of mythic identity, when he noted he was not Hercules, but Atlas. This man had been a terror in the hospital, being passed from ward to ward because of dangerousness made more overt by a giant size and extreme ways, exemplified when he attacked personnel with the shaft of his fractured humerus. He took readily to the Ward 10 therapeutic community as caretaker, reflective of a messianic aspect of his character. Joining the discussion on mythic terms is reflective of a personality organized in a manner in which he could be stated to be his own grandparent, alongside readiness to regress to being his own grandchild, both evidence of alienation from self.

The group took a further step forward in arriving at a conjunction of messianism and psychopathy, Mosha's self-immolation and Marsten's avaricious rule over others and their possessions. Mosha felt responsible for all, punishing self for his lack, and Marsten felt that all belonged to him.

Ten Months In

Ten months after inception of the group, the group had arrived to the point where a member was able to engage in open discussion of his pre-assaultiveness, stemming from persecutory delusions (the voice of his girlfriend in his head) that were relieved by open discussion in the group. Secretive members, like Pimental, communicated their inner nadir, or ultimately low states, by staring like a deer in the headlights, commented on by members.

Jones, who had been a leading antisocial member, on the way to court testified to his conversion. He waxed positive about his new feeling of self-esteem and relaxation. The members joined in approaching the Marsten-Waleed feud, in which both claimed the other was a bully. Waleed admitted to a Rambo status.

Edwards vividly enacted an underlying low self-esteem he characterized as "a piece of shit," not caring whether he lived or died. Waleed enacted that low state, followed by members' pride in their capacity to help one another. Figueroa was exuberant about the helpfulness of his medication. The members testified to the group's helpfulness. It had now been meeting for a year.

This was followed by a scene where Gutierrez stood on a chair, making a political speech, eventually recounting Mexican losses in Western USA. Underlying and inherent leadership came to the fore, expressing itself first in an autistic fashion (as when Gutierrez ascended the chair to right old wrongs and carry on past causes) versus working through dilemmas of his own. He displayed a new-found love for America at the end of that episode.

Waleed and Horvathton engaged in a feud, accusing each other of aggression, which was commented on by the members as puerile. The group serves a useful purpose in mediating these friction points, and analyzes the immature and psychopathic character of the members. The group is firmly established as a forum of opinion. Also, music played an increasing role, under the ministrations of the Music Therapist. Work in a previous correctional setting, Howard Hall at St. Elizabeth's Hospital, resulted in formation by the patients of an orchestra, which played for the larger therapeutic community. Here the playing of music and singing was a weekly function, led by the music therapist and myself. Prominent there was the song Hotel California. Also, members danced with me.

The members returned to discussion of the old prison code, ending in a constructive discussion of the alteration of problem children, with Moran identifying himself as such. They previously had agreed to talk through the Waleed-Horvathton conflict, versus fisticuffs. Delgado and Laws engaged in emotional inquiry in their suicidal intentions, ending on a warm note. This was the most extensive essay of the group into the interpersonal and intrapsychic dynamics of a member, attesting to the maturity of the group. Personnel and patients joined freely. Consensus was that Laws was overly dependent on his girlfriend. Faith in self was urged, a borderline messianic concept.

The group had advanced to a capacity for intuitive connectedness, spontaneous exposition of what was on their minds, systematic inquiry into their crimes. These were sufficient for passing the CAT test, and autonomous inquiry into their situations of alienation from self and others, to prepare for reconciliation. The administrative personnel continued cooperation with the treatment team, in managing a series of very difficult patients, the unit participating in hospital-wide colloquia on Therapeutic Community.

Ward 10's Living In Reality Group, a Summary

This was a subgroup of the therapeutic community with a mandate to aid its members to live in reality. Participants volunteered for membership which also generally included individual therapy with me. It met once per week for an hour. The task of the program was preparing the patients to appear in court to defend themselves. But basic to that was their problem with reality, hence the name of the group. Basic to that was their problem with themselves, their ego problems. The ward psychiatrist's instructions to the members included keeping their seats, speaking to the subject, and supporting one another related to their ego problems.

The sessions of this group are detailed in volume two (please see Appendices A2 and B2.) The group began in April of 1990 and ended in April of 1994.

The ward psychiatrist and I co-led the group, and at the same time he was in training in such leadership. He started it by defining its parameters, chiefly relating to behavior. A member directly asked if it would be held against him if he walked out of the group. The ward psychiatrist replied that it would not. In turn, I emphasized equity and authentic self-expression by asking the members to go the rounds on what was on their minds. Alonzo Smith started what turned out to be a course in self-revelation, starting with a subjective corset-like feeling of pressure that he ascribed to his confinement. He then related it to missing his son. That led to an exposition by a hebephrenic member, about his wishes to reform himself; then Alonzo engaged in the first intuitive connection with the group, about an out of body experience, itself related to his tie with his son. This was followed by a dream about defending his wife and son against assault. Later he noted her betrayal of him and his giving up his life for her. Gold sobbed about his father's failure to care for his family. A member asked how one becomes one-self, and another member asserted his lack of capacity to cry, versus a machine-like state.

We were encouraged by the forthcoming nature of the members, their readiness to share their bodily awareness, dream life, and life course issues, but above all, Alonzo Smith's capacity for initiating intuitive connection related to an out-of-body experience. Rocco and Estes followed that lead, Estes noting he had flying dreams. Heywood Smith, Martin, Snodgrass, and Muston said they had that too, and there was much conviviality over that.

Alonzo Smith brought up a dream in which he defended his wife and son against a group that was threatening. The ward psychiatrist supported him for his defending his family. Estes brought out a dream in which he thought that something chasing him almost caught up to him. He switched the dream. Earlier, Rocco asked what flying dreams meant. I said that they meant one was transcending a threat, getting on top of it, and noted that the dream had to do with some threat arising inside the individual, defending against it and catching up with one. The group ended at this point.

Afterwards, a clump of patients persisted. Rocco asked to talk with me, revealing an obsession with his mother, who he said had sexually assaulted him. He had tried suicide by drowning at 4 ½ and 5. She reportedly said she would drive him crazy, punish him if he told anyone. He did not know about being a crazy man, except that he was afraid.

Alonzo then came out with a messianic message. He mentioned his wife and her betrayal of him. He asserted that he gave his life for her. Heywood Smith responded that he would not give his life for anyone, that he would go to a nudist camp, pick up a woman, then transact in a swinging group. Rocco began to laugh about women. A member responded with tirades about his past life. Alonzo was straightforward about a wish to become a minister, with black clothes, to teach his child good behavior.

In the next session, a member closer to reality asked for a kitchen job, and another cited his hope for himself. Then, with Rocco in the lead, the members, intuitively connected, explored the issue of giving in to punitive authority. Munston citing as he put it, "spent 13 years in Dr. Abrahams," in which he indicated his alienation from himself in favor of the other. Patient Smith discussed offering his life messianically, while Gold cited the reality of life, and the need to face reality.

Next, the members turned isolative, and on being rounded up by myself, explored their intrapsychic life, alienation from self, and subsequent craziness. Darrow's recent dramatic display of crisis regarding his manhood was central there. Alonzo prayed for Rocco' self-feeling, Martin revealed his altruistic career in caring for delinquent youth, and Paul's experience with ghosts. Alonzo then related a spell of alienation on his mother's part, and the role of Christ in their reconciliation. In the next session, members related morbid family conflicts, Gold sobbing about his and his father's failures, stating he was no longer macho, and could cry.

The members settled into an existential state of identity diffusion, where horseplay was prominent, speaking in schizophrenese, citing a lost feeling. Healy encountered his sadness re a suicide at age 10. Casales related his suicidal attempt by hanging, experiencing his father as an apparition. In a later session, Casales suggested talking about mother, citing kidnapping a prostitute from her pimp. Smith noted his closeness to his mother, later attesting that closeness to his son. Members cited addiction to drugs as related to need for closeness and safety. The ward psychiatrist cited members who missed their voices.

Four months after the inception of the group, members began to cite the relationship of their crimes to their mental state, Smith citing a hole inside. A former member dramatically told his story of breaking his back, transferring to intellectual pursuits. Smith noted his own evil insides, still alive. Members cited their careers in alienation. Moran, the chief alienated other, asked to rejoin the group, and was conditionally allowed to do so. Smith, more serious about therapy, cited the alienation of his wife, also from himself.

Six months after the inception of the group, Moran, previously isolative and incoherent, spoke clearly about his crime and antisocial tendency, and members began unburdening. Alonzo Smith reported that his mother's personality was within him, beating him down, versus being human. In succeeding sessions he and others went into their openly psychotic episodes, involving haunts by dead family members.

Moran remarked on what members got out of life, leading to prolonged discussion of self-realization and one's ideals. Moran gave away that which he liked, cigarettes. A year after the inception of the group, he engaged in a prolonged exposition of his life on the edge of society. At that time the shift lead, who had been antagonistic to therapeutic community attended the group, to cite his introversion as a handicap as group leader, and an earlier, successful experience in leading a group. Members went on to discuss their hallucinations, also near death experiences.

Powdermaker turned reflective of the schizophrenia of the others, who might kill otherwise. Members, particularly Ruelas, cited alienation from family as causative. Spellman openly mourned his mother. A red light resulted from a mutual assault by Weninger and Calendar. Members discussed the different realities they live in. Weninger related about his crime family, grandiose self, murderous father. Nikka exemplified that life course. Members, including Calendar, discussed their lost professional aspirations. They were positive about their professional care, inner problems, one calling it a "broken insides" state of death. Flores attributed his temper to his father's death, and Powdermaker was driven to insomnia by the loss of his father.

The sessions became increasingly coherent, devoted to helping members with problems such as Glass's violent temper and Swayze's victimization by a girl. Also Callahan's and Dressler's tie to their families, their depression over it, connected to failure regarding one of their CAT tests.

Summary Individual Therapy on Ward 10

It would take another book to present the protocols of the individual therapy entered into by the patients of Ward 10. Instead, I have selected one patient I consider representative. He was a long-term patient, sunk in psychosis and psychopathy, who nevertheless displayed affect sufficient to engage with me intuitively. He was actively hallucinating, hypomanic, unable to keep his mind on the questions incident to the training course to fit him for appearance in court. His cognitive assets were mobilized in the Therapeutic Community and Living In Reality Groups, and he "got the idea" of what it meant to live in reality. The prior and ongoing group experience served to mobilize, guide, and support him as he reached out to me and his peers, and he took counsel with himself on his immediate and life course issues, but as his individual sessions will show, it became evident that it was the individual relationship that did all of that and more.

It is in the details of the therapeutic course that these essential changes became apparent. The reader is referred to those details in the account given in the appendix under the rubric A3: A Detailed Account Individual Therapy: Patient Sucras.

Sucras is a 33-year-old white male, determined as unable to stand trial, pursuant to Section 1370. While a patient at Napa, he allegedly assaulted a staff member. He was diagnosed as suffering from schizophrenic disorder with a paranoid chronic nature, alcohol abuse, and borderline intellectual functioning. Placed on psychotropic medication to ameliorate psychotic symptomatology, he was transferred to Ward 10, the Trial Competency Program. He was first formally assessed on May 13, 1991, with unsatisfactory performance. He was noticeably hypomanic with a management problem.

Sucras was found to be very intrusive, dependent and needy. Regarding his capacity to stand trial, he had a basic appreciation of the proceedings against him, but limited ability to cooperate. His intellectual limitations were obvious, consisting of fixation on internal stimuli. He was referred to schooling in a mock trial. That consisted of a true or false pretest on the roles of courtroom officials, followed by a mock competency hearing. On August 9th, 1991, he attended a pretest. After months of instruction and encouragement, he then attended mock trial. On March 6th, 1992 he attended and successfully completed the mock trial activity. He passed the oral pretest with 70%, and was admitted to a mock competency hearing. On the witness stand in mock trial, his speech was pressured and he was obviously nervous. He stated that he was ill on the day of the alleged crime. His illness was cited as "being ready to go off with the voices."

He was not assaultive at this hospital and appeared content to return to this facility as an insane patient. He understood the consequences and ramifications of the insanity defense, as well as the various pleas and plea bargains. Because of his disability, he needed to be returned to court for conservatorship. He consented to be interviewed, and wished to return to court. He volunteered: "I've been here a long time and I've not physically assaulted anybody." He felt he was doing fine and was ready to stand trial. He had acknowledged that he could come back to the hospital and go to another unit if he pled not guilty by reason of insanity.

According to the defendant, "I was insane and was hearing voices and I was seeing things at the time of the crime." He went on to state that he spent almost 17 years in a state institution and felt that he would do additional time, most likely at this hospital, if he was found insane. He was willing to take medication. At this time he would need

51

psychiatric placement to ensure completion of the trial process. He has been in this hospital almost a year without an assault, and is maintained on his current medication. These were an antipsychotic; Navane, 10 mg per day; Amitriptyline, 75 mg per day; Lithium Carbonate, 100 mg per day; and Valproic acid, 1500 mg per day.

Background: Patient's father died at age 59 of TB and emphysema when patient was nine. He was a tool and die maker. Patient had a 10th grade education. The patient tells a story of a mother engaged in prostitution on his bed. She threw him out when he protested. Another story was that she evicted him from the home at age 17 when she caught him masturbating.

She resorted to calling the police when he assaulted her. He also committed arson, resulting in his residence in Juvenile Hall in 1974. Then, at age 16, he was hospitalized at Napa State Hospital, where he earned a GED. He raped a female patient there, threatening her with a knife to her throat. His mother was placed in Agnew State Hospital. The patient was at Atascadero State Hospital in 1983, followed by three more admissions.

Patient exhibited both psychomotor retardation and acceleration. He was disoriented in relation to time. In three previous psychological assessments, intellectual function was deemed borderline. Patient stated, "My schizophrenia started when I was hit in the head, at age 5."

Sucras was born in San Francisco and raised in Santa Rosa. His mother was depressed about her father's death. Her mother abused him with a rolling pin, knocking him unconscious. The patient's grandmother died while he was in Napa, and left him $20,000. There were many occasions of suicide attempts and he was arrested for arson on three occasions. Patient was also preoccupied with a homosexual relationship, but could not tolerate relationships. He stated he was a psychiatric technician and did not have to take medications.

The initial task here was establishment of a therapeutic alliance. In the TC and Living In Reality Groups, he showed leadership in making representation, though of a negative nature, but still engaging with me in dialogue. I invited him to see me in my office, and he accepted. Sucras's history of continuing his schooling while at Napa State Hospital was a good sign; he was evidently of higher intelligence than the borderline finding. Also, alongside a hebephrenic cast to his verbal production, I sensed depression, which I set to explore. I soon found him to be capable of establishing a positive emotional tie, simultaneous with a playful assaultiveness.

He started by asking me what he should talk about. I answered that it would be what came to his mind. He then drew a stick figure on the blackboard, oriental, silly smile, stating that he was once happy because he had a girlfriend. He then stated that he needed to be "unwound." He had assumed the role of a student, in play therapy. The next hour he was playfully ritualistic and jocular, and reported a dream of a woman located on Ward 9, (possibly at Napa hospital) who had died. He thought of her as a witch.

I thought of him as a warlock; later he characterized himself as a desperado, somehow related to Jesus. His language tended to schizophrenese, tending to low self-esteem, manifesting messianism, as well a fixation on the woman he had raped in Napa. He then induced the first intuitive connection with me, related to fear, which he stated was rife among the patients. He then dreamed of a witch/mother, mopping the floor, then he was aware of a resemblance between me and his father.

I inferred that the relationship was sufficient for the transference (that from the past which interfered with the capacity to experience the present) to appear. It took the form of a dream of atomic devastation, followed by death and resurrection as spirits. The night nurse became apprehensive that the patient would go "off." However, he instead moved into a form of intimacy with me by playfully throwing paper at me. He persisted until I became annoyed, citing we would have to cut back on our hours. He then relented. Afterwards he reported that he had lived in a garbage can and identified with a girl in coitus. He added that he had dreamed of millions of mice falling from the sky.

Several sessions later he reported that he had TB, like his father. At the same time, he openly acted like an appealing naughty child, then a serious adult. He drew female genitalia, citing awareness that he was sick, a nobody, wanted to get well, and was affiliated with me. He was sad about being "crazy in the morning", trying to find himself. He admitted to a homosexual identity, and was determined to let go of the hedonic aspects of his delusions.

Sucras wanted to go back to college, then picked up the paper he threw at me. Eight months after beginning the individual therapy, he soberly addressed his sad life, and wished for a dignified one. He went further, to state that he had given up on himself when his father died, citing trying to bring him back and the impossibility of mourning him. He did not want to leave ASH and had been resisting taking the CAT test. The dreams of psychic death were recurrent.

He admitted to loving being crazy and reported an inner war over reality. Then he saw a white light, all was dark, and the doctor was dead. He laughed when someone was in pain, it was a nightmare in his head. He had an impulsion to steal my cassettes. He characterized self as a paramecium, born from an anus. He stated he cries nightly about his dad. The voices he had heard were fading and had stopped tapping his head. He was more settled within himself to talk like a man, saying no "kiddie talk." Patient then returned to the issue of his mother's belief in Christ, his own, and enacted assault on my head with a manila envelope. I took offense and ordered him out. He had reported in an earlier hour a radio assault on his brain. He reported a dream at 5 of having sex with a girl. Navane calms down his sexuality, but he feels dead without this sex. Sucras had changed his mind about leaving the hospital; now wanted to do so and to take the test. He also wished to pray. Life came to be through his genitals, along with intuitive connection. He noted thinking of a skyscraper being torn down, in favor of a plaza. Finally, he was getting his life together, looking forward to leaving the hospital. Then he cited that he hated men and loved only women. Faced with his victim in court, he cried. Patient was aware of having a damaged brain, but "still can't think straight." He is looking forward to "working at a job."

In an effort to work on himself, he cited that he talks a lot to avoid hearing Satan. He also reported experiencing God. He is starting to sleep, but cries when he is treated well. Patient had walked out in anger over medication management, requesting termination of lithium. He was still fearful of leaving the hospital. Each night he died in his sleep, then came back to life. Inside his head he feels hurt when people are dying. He was the Devil, dying himself.

The patient began having dreams of reconciliation, turning to God, attending Mass and fighting voices which told him to kill himself. He was now able recognize his delusions, also his feminine identity. The treatment team recommended that he continue to see a psychiatrist, and return to school when he leaves the hospital. On his father's death, he had designated him as the man of the family. Patient expected himself to do well in school, "once he gets sex out of his head."

A year after beginning his therapy, Sucras reported that his fellows in TC were anxious about his passing the testing, and supportive of his improvement. He was crying; "If I can find out my problems and answer my own questions, that is a sign of getting well. Will I be sick the rest of my life?" He agreed to communicate with the doctor after he left the hospital.

Commentary

This man had been hospitalized for 19 years and alienated from his mother, then was given to arson and multiple suicidal attempts. He lived the life of an isolate, hallucinating and delusional. On Ward 10, he had formed attachments to members in the Therapeutic Community and the Living In Reality groups, but the most significant attachment had been to me, one analogous to his father, and to his schooling.

In the hours with me, he became childlike, engaging in games he devised, including throwing paper. I lent myself to that game, monitoring my involvement as a sign of his, and at several times placing limits, which he accepted. He proved himself capable of free association, including dream analysis. It evoked transference material having to do with his attachment to his father, and mourning his (father's) death, plus his own psychic death, and resurrection. He reported improvement in his capacity for restorative sleep. Hopeful, he began to struggle with his delusions and hallucinations, envisioning the assumption and resumption of a relatively normal life. The patient, Sucras, was severely hallucinating, hypomanic, and unable to keep his mind on the questions incident to the training course traversed by his peers. His cognitive assets have been mobilized in the Therapeutic Community and Living In Reality groups, but not to the extent induced by the individual to individual sessions. The self-report is more detailed and searching, inducing deeper involvement of the analyst.

Therapeutic Community Ward 24: A Schematic Summary

As in the presentation of the development of therapeutic community on Ward 10, we here shall summarize, winnowing the data down in accordance with the criteria of therapeutic community. A full protocol can be found in Appendix D. The challenge on Ward 10 rested with fitting acutely ill forensic patients for trial. The emphasis on Ward 10 lay in recovery of cognitive capacity—to understand their charges and the nature of their crimes—but the avenue towards that recovery lay in the therapeutic alliance, in the reestablishment of emotional connection. The patients chosen for the Ward 24 experiment had been ill for periods ranging from several to twelve years, generally already adjudicated as insane and therefore not guilty. But they were on indefinite detention, pending recovery. Ahead lay successful tenure at another state mental hospital.

In contrast to Ward 10, the personnel, administrative and treatment team were chosen for their acceptance of the therapeutic community in concept and in practice. The patients were chosen principally for their presumed capacity for dormitory life, since there were no single rooms, except for several devoted to isolation. As on 10, the regimen of the therapeutic community group involved roll call, announcements, engagement in the game of trivial pursuit, and finally general discussion time. First on that agenda were problems that had arisen since the last meeting.

In the initial session, the members first asked me what I wanted to discuss. I answered that I wanted to talk, like human beings, about what was on their minds. At that crucial moment, Russel walked to the front of the room, to tell of his Mafia origin. Another member, Casales, stood up and reported that the members tended to act as bullies. Another member, Marino, accused Casales of calling him a bully, getting up to fight when Casales denied he did. Marino escalated to the point of requiring full bed restraints. I noted that examples of why people fought were springing up all over the room. Members, smiling, agreed. A member complained that another was spitting on the floor, in a corner. I turned to him, asking him if he was ready to fight. He replied that he was, if needed, despite his age of 72.

This turned out to be the critical transaction of the session, through which I reached the group. In the next session, members Wilson and Valliant reached out to us, followed by Gordon, seeking to organize an activities program. Then in the next session, Phillips plunged into psychotherapy proper, referring to his twisted emotional state. The members began discussion of their racism.

Members began griping, in a borderline manner, but also cooperatively about their self-governance. Gordon, maintaining a prosocial stance, started a long struggle with authority about his ostensibly inadequate treatment, which culminated in disgorgement a year later of a dramatic murder of his common law wife. In subsequent sessions, the members grew increasingly positive about their Therapeutic Community. They were learning to discuss who they were and what they want from TC.

Character Analysis Begins

Seven months after inception of the group, the members began to inquire about the authoritarian and rebellious aspects of each other's characters. Gordon began it, responded to by Valliant, and followed by Phillips. Gordon bullied the members in the service of reforming them, acting martyred when they reciprocated. Valliant exemplified this by citing that Gordon acted like a kid who had been raped. Reports of members weeks moved over to an AA-like self-report on alienated and emotional states of being. Hylton reported his suicidal state when betrayed by his father, and Valliant his estrangement from women, edging into his life course.

Self-conscious change was broached, along with a long-term attempt to change Corker, an obdurately alienated member who professed that it would take a long time to change him; that people had tried without success. The members became silent and intuitively connected, after which Gordon reported that he was in tears.

This was a critical session, in which I defined the task of the group regarding specific problems of individuals, identifying changes they needed to make, and how to go about them. The problem in motivation came first, then change, and then feedback.

The members regressed psychically towards trust of one another and the group process; they regressed into awareness of formally alienated aspects of their personality. This was a hopeful development, exhibiting an emotional dialectic of thesis-antithesis-synthesis, with deeper entry into their selves as persons. Corker represented a challenge to the group, with his alienating defenses, combined with psychopathic charm. The silence was of great significance, as I had learned from previous work at Fort Knox and St. Elizabeth's.

Another event of intuitive connection followed, with Phillips volunteering data regarding a sick relationship with his victim, leading to further revelation by him and others of their states of alienation and crimes. There were indications of altered ego states, secondary to lessened psychopathy. This was marked by sensations of head spinning and open spirituality. Eight months after inception, a member, Valliant, intuitively connected and reported reconciliation with an estranged brother whom he had brutalized. Another reported assaulting his father; and Corker, who had held he was normal, reported he was too sick for the group. Patrick, who was previously committed to violence and psychopathy, announced hope for his future. At the end of December, members debated on changing one's personality, with Valliant and Gordon later responding positively. Boulware reported feeling sick and hallucinatory, but in a manner receptive to the group's help. Resistance to giving in was exemplified by Corker and Phillips, interpreted by Gordon.

Phillips, then intuitively connected, reported grieving his mother, who had died of cancer, leading others to identify with him. Valliant again reported reconciling with his brother, and, remorseful, again emphasized how he had been antisocial when first locked up.

Members intervened in a conflict between Moran and Colander, who intended to kill one another. Moran later revealed a dream of death of his mother, and a nighttime encounter with the Deity. Corker, empathetic, later described his private hell. Valliant reported his self-punitiveness for his evil tendencies. Then there was a session in which members, including the doctor, were intuitively connected over aloneness and a wish to belong.

In one session, Gordon burst forth with a vivid, disjointed account of the murder of his wife, whom he suspected of having an affair with a neighbor. Alonzo and Sanger responded, asserting the reality of what was going on. This was followed by session in which members reported loss of reality, evil and dead states, abandonment by a parental figure, and alienation from self. Gordon reported his remorse in a later session.

When I announced I was going on a summer vacation, the members were supportive, stating they wished to work with a favorite nurse, as they had with me. They recognized their contrariness, and Corker advocated natural cooperativeness. Gordon was beset by flashbacks from the past. Figueroa edged towards reconciliation with his family. Corker reported the doctor's resemblance to his father.

Members like Abana, intuitively connected, brought up their voyages in self-knowledge. Hopkins cited his regression into depression, induced by Keith Corker, who in turn accepted reflection of himself as "superioristic." In identification, I experienced intuitive connection and vertigo, in which I fell downwards. Corker revealed awareness of a life sentence since childhood.

Valliant, further re-bonding with his brother, relates pain of loss of those who had worshipped him. Alonzo asserted there was "no way out but the production of a new society," yet noted he had improved. Gordon gave further evidence of his own bull-headedness, a problem with manhood. Moran realized his alienation and obnoxiousness. Valliant realized his self-sabotage. Corker saw no hope for self. Alonzo and Valliant saw self as perfectionist, like Corker.

Members further admitted to their narcissistic ways. Taylor and Bushman talked schizophrenese about attacking a woman. Corker cited difficulty in separating self from his past, saw self as a cockroach through the doctor's eyes. Later, he stated the voices pounded away. Bushman speculated that they were from God. Dormer cited that voices were fixated in his brain, and Blakely that they show sin and guilt. Corker stated he had difficulty taking a helping hand.

While Valliant realized he needed to sink back into therapy in the face of his regression into paranoia, itself impelled by an imperative for positive response, the members, intuitively connected, proceeded with exposition of their needs. They talked about their problematic selves, going mental about their feelings, and back and forth about therapy. Corker significantly "took it," when criticized for monopolizing the phone and TV. Crying about the loss of friends, he then discussed his need for restraints.

Valliant led the members in self-inquiry, saying "I can do it without acting up," as had Corker and Gordon, who engaged in further exposition of his crime. The session turned tumultuous. The members intuitively connected with me re my birthday. Corker cited he was thinking of his insides and denied he was king anymore.

In the last session, Valliant took initiative, indicating how open he was in the trailers. Sensing his need for approbation, yet aiming towards further work on his driven narcissism, I remarked on his idealism. He then opened up on his fear of confrontation, were he to really open up, expecting to drive the doctor to unprofessionalism. In referring to people looking down at him, he was indicating fixation at a low, alienated state. I intuited that he was talking about vengeance, and asked for confirmation. He asserted perceiving that in the here and now.

Carrying the free associational dynamic a step further and exemplifying what Valliant perceived, Cantor entered the fray, bringing in the ego ideal factor of fairness, verging on revelation of the life circumstance that led him to feel life was unfair, and how he had altered his alienating ways. Valliant referred to his life course as a 12–13 year course of losing his temper.

I brought up Corker 's current problem in that regard, and he reassured me of a change in himself, a willingness to adapt. Then, importantly, Valliant cited his jealousy re a nurse, also a social worker, and a revelatory statement about sentencing to death the offender. To me that indicated a still devoutly held schizoid position. Sanger cited his identity with that, in regard to his history with his father in his youth, later asserting identity with the therapeutic alliance. Moran then began the process of opening himself to the therapeutic dialog on the unit.

The schizoid position we encountered in Valliant's subjectivity apparently stemmed from transcendence of mythic nature. He was protector as well as executioner.

The members at the end of this work appeared to be actively engaged with the therapist and one another and improving. As evidence of that in the analysis of the patient Valliant, his realization of commitment to an autistic, and out of this world idealistic position from which he held both himself and others responsible. This was analogous to the out-of-this-world position held by a leader of the group in ward 10, Darrow. Analysis of this idealistic position gave promise of recovery from this man's malady. Along the way, he and his fellows were guiding one another towards such recovery.

Summary: Ward 24's Living In Reality Group

The members of this group were voluntary, recruited from the Ward 24 therapeutic community. Given the mandate as a group to explore and affirm the sense of reality of its members, in relation to common reality, it generally had six to eight members. They met for an hour twice weekly beginning in May of 1994 and ending in July of 1996. Most sought individual therapy with me as well.

As in the therapeutic community group, the members were enjoined to say what came to mind. In the first session, Phillips idealized the doctor, asserted his ancestral lineage, and Valliant commented on Phillips' grandiosity as proportional to his low self-esteem. Guido then brought up the issue of multiple realities; Elias said his was determined by his evolving goals. Valliant cited society's role in determining sickness, also one's family's ideals and upbringing. Yardley reported on his subjective sense of being "dumped on." Valliant reported on his crazy spells, 13 years of them, also involving a feeling of being a scapegoat. A member reported on his alienation and bitterness. Phillips ended the session by observing that the members each carried grudges. In sum, the members had idealized the therapy, displaying grandiosity; then they edged into feelings of injustice and victimization, and began telling their stories, led by Valliant and Phillips.

In the next session, still identifying with the therapy, the members were led by Phillips, who characterized its work as a bottomless pit, then the members complained of being treated unfairly, and one cited his isolative way as putting his dresser to the wall. In the next session, the members entered into intuitive connection, initiating accounts of their problematic stories involving alienation from themselves and their families.

A third session was begun by Phillips on his drug history and how he's now straight; followed by a member who cited his own jealousy. Valliant exemplified an inner despair since childhood, with temper outbursts, panics, and tendency to violence. One session was interrupted by an emergency TC session, occasioned by discovery of the absence of a number of bedsprings. The members of this group reacted with a display of arrogant anger, led by Valliant. Phillips led with accounts of their deviance. Roberts identified Wilson as "a tough Gorber with feelings," and Wilson arrived at a feeling of conceit in his head. The members regressed to prison ways in the following session, then to one in which Hopkins became a centerpiece about his wish to kill his father. Abana, Valliant, and Cunningham identified with him, while Yardley dis-identified and walked out. Boulware started in on the issue of flatus brought up by Corker. He in the next session asked for discussion of his rivalry with another member, then admitted to his getting mad.

Eight Months In

Eight months after inception of the group, Valliant, partnering with Phillips, intuitively connected, then advanced in reconciliation with his father. Phillips advanced to an account of the commission of his crime. Members very moved.

Moran included, members confronted Capp, a leader of an antisocial gang, prison psychology group, re his feud with Moran. It was a constructive outcome. This was a crucial event, in which Capp exemplified the group's problem with male violent transformation combined with identification with a malevolently oriented father figure. He followed Patrick in being the baby and judge of the group, who engaged in an *ad hominem* exchange, reporting internal processes, in transferentially-loaded fashion.

The group transmuted into a prosocial gang, the members collaborated and competed in telling on themselves. Phillips characterized the sessions by citing them as a movie, with different stories. The members, at Moran's instance, discussed his problems in fitting in to their family, with focus by Gordon at the end on homosexuality. Phillips and others tell a story of high, then low feelings. Maintaining an easy going atmosphere, members mollified Moran, potentially enraged by an insult communicated through his mother. A red light was averted, in confrontation of Corker and Moran re baby-sitting him, and his homosexuality, his underlying identity. Moran was criticized for his childish ways, for being self-centered; Gordon dreamed of killing something, taking eggs from chicks. Sanger asked for help with his pain. Next came a rambling session, on being good at mother's instance. Corker relented in his alienation from the doctor.

A year after inception of the group, Gordon asserted a therapeutic goal of dealing with his arrogance; Callahan was criticized by the members for being cut off from them and his self.

The members reacted to a suicide on another ward, culminated in a statement by Moran, dialectical, regarding faulting the suicidee, and Moran's seeking help on the death of his father recently. The members discussed pride in self, standards, and lowering them, letting things fall into place. Patrick was counseled by members about his fight, and subsequent full-bed restraints. Alonzo testified for medication. In a session marked first by intuitive connection, the members slipped into schizophrenese, indicating their apprehension about confrontation with psychopathic prisoners. Corker exemplified one in an episode with me. Patrick, exemplifying for the group, opened up about his impulsive action, and revealed he was acting like his father. Valliant admitted to following that course, and now changed, feels better.

Next came a seminal session, in which members associated to and exemplified each other's production, denoting alienation from self and parents to criminal status. The theories of motivation, root cause, spoiling by parents, and silver spoon status were discussed. Phillips, Valliant, Abana, Patrick and Corker responded to Moran's call for help, denoting his evil and good sides, with Corker at the end exemplifying the negative. Members discussed giving in to accepting mundane reality. Corker and others helped Moran away from seclusion to trust; away from violence to self-management.

Another seminal session, stemming from dreams by Moran, involved haunts, interpreted by members as fear of leaving the hospital. Corker followed that with a paradoxical statement that being locked up was his freedom. Valliant and Bushman followed that with their long term states of alienation, and basic self-transformation in therapy. Corker engaged with them regarding his handicap—controlling parents—and his blue baby status. Dormer identifies with him. Then in another seminal session, Bushman exemplified a tie to a maternal object, messianic in nature, and she ambivalent. This was followed by a fragmented session, culminating in exemplification by Bushman of dysfunctional family, and a love tie to his alcoholic mother.

Members were striving to get to self-reality, from being cut off from self. The nurse supervisor led members in exploration of family history, differentiation from its influence, to selfhood. In a seminal exercise, members came to the conclusion that what they see of reality is governed by their belief systems, key to the racist divide. Bushman, in complete denial, wished off the unit, exemplified by members, especially one whose father had death wishes, then Bushman spoke of his mental illness. He continued in the next session, brainwashed himself to intuitive connection, caretaking. Santos broke in with his marital imbroglio and his crazy wife, leading to Gordon's revelation that he had killed his. This was followed by a disjointed session regarding mother as prostitute, and the commitment of crime while hating one's mother.

Members then bought up the issue of long time alienation from self, and the handling of such. In his individual hours, Gordon systematically explored his crime, and the alienation from self that led to his state of paranoia and the central part that it played in committing it.

On scrutiny the members here extended their inquiry into self in the therapeutic community more deeply. They appeared to be holding one another to the task, leading the reader into the worlds of the schizophrenic and psychopath, then back to reality. The reader is urged to consult with Appendix D for further details on this exciting venture.

Summary Individual Therapy: Patient Valliant

This patient was chosen, from the 24 members treated, for his representative qualities in exemplifying what went on in his individual therapy. He had been hospitalized for 17 years, and while he did not give evidence of hallucination, was sufficiently delusional as to have murdered the guinea pigs he was commissioned to care for. He also was alienated from his family and generally from his peers. On the positive side, he had engaged for some months in individual therapy on a previous ward.

This 38-year-old white male had been under treatment at ASH for 13 years, as a Mentally Disordered Sex Offender. In his instant offense he had viciously imprisoned and raped a woman. There were several previous rapes, abuse of alcohol, and a robbery. His behavioral aberration began at age 6, when his parents divorced and the five children were farmed out to foster homes. Wild destructive episodes proved to be a management problem, and he was recurrently institutionalized, starting at age seven. He was eventually diagnosed as bipolar, alcohol-dependent, and sexually sadistic, with borderline personality disorder. He had done best on risperidone and lithium. The risperidone calmed him and allayed periods of paranoid thinking. The lithium slowed his rushed thinking and evened his moods. Up to his residence on Ward 24, his therapy had consisted largely of anger management and Alcoholics Anonymous. He and his family were alienated from one another.

A dynamic he reported in his history, of managing his siblings at his mother's instance, became manifest in his participation in Therapeutic Community and Living In Reality groups. He eagerly sought the systematic individual appointments I offered the ward population. There he diligently reported what came to his mind, including his dreams and fantasies. We began meeting in May of 1994.

This patient readily formed a therapeutic alliance. He was a pro-social leader in the Therapeutic Community group, also the Living In Reality group. He launched into his material without needing prompting on my part. He had tried to talk with psychiatrists along the way, gleaning data on himself, amounting to the fact that he was his own worst enemy. He furnished the datum that the she who was coming back was his mother, who visited him at his first foster home, stating she would return in two weeks, and never did. He went on to state that this was behind his wild rages.

In his second hour, he made representations about my note-taking in an appropriate, non-paranoid manner. I would say that the hindrance was the aspect of his character that yelled at God and Jesus. Regarding his strong belief in God and Jesus, I welcomed that sentiment as messianic, and possibly developing as part of a therapeutic alliance with me. I also welcomed his capacity for insight into his emotional innards. "He's [Jesus] not inside me." I looked for psychoanalytic introjects which bound the patient to sickness. A profound tie to his maternal object was the most likely candidate.

In his third hour he presented a dream of a football game, with a 10-year-old girl at the center of opposition. It got spooky, in which he chopped off hands and heads, ran to a touchdown, a nightmare of body parts inside the football, with cannibalism on the patient's part. He associated to a feeling of impossibility at making it with a woman.

This seminal dream exemplified data about this man's regressive tendencies, also a possible course back to reality from his regressive fixation. On the thesis that everything in the dream is the dreamer, it posed the thesis of a feminine identity alongside heroic masculinity, achieving a touchdown. The spooky part exemplified the catastrophic centerpiece in his development, centering about the breakup of his family, and his tie with his mother. He also engaged in a dialogue with himself about basic motivation and his doubts in regards to his masculinity. He hints at it with the miracle of successful courtship with a normal girl, an achievement which could act as a platform for an analysis of his morbidity.

The next session started with the patient almost talking schizophrenese. It related to his spiritual side, a clue to his spiritual tie with the mother within. There was a disassociation from his rational self, that comprehends. Alcohol aided in alleviating the blockade, and played a part in his rapes, the comprehension of his underlying motivation. Mid-session, he reached to cognition of his tie with his mother, and importantly, experienced intuitive connection with me, also his father, and dirtiness. It was glommed together with his heavenly tie with his mother, locked into its incestuous specialness. It is of note that she slapped before she cuddled.

In the next hour, he declared that he was both judge and executioner, in relation to his crime and his murder of animals. In a previous therapy, in analysis of his tie with his mother, he regressed to conceiving of himself as a werewolf. He apologized for the rage he experienced toward me, related to injustice. I inferred that the affective mobilization of the therapy brought the patient into awareness of rage towards me, as a transference towards the maternal object. The injustice he referred to stems from his mother's ego ideal of an out-of-this-world mutuality. It appeared in the next hour that his mother had betrayed their mutuality by a relationship with a black man.

It appeared that he became angry in the family problems group; Valliant was irritated by the God aspect of AA, quite possibly due to rivalry. He referred to a tantrum, linking it to his crime of rape. His soul's mission in his therapy is linking together the pieces of self-loathing by his associations. Prominent there was a family relevant mission of reconciliation with his brothers and father. Concomitant was a parapsychological (see glossary) alienation from being "momma's good boy." When he came to ASH, his family and father had told him that to them, he was dead. From prodigal son, he was plunged into nadirhood, deserving death. He went on to cite his problem with passion, as with his mother, killing the hamsters on Ward 6. He exploded for 25 minutes and they could not get him down. He said it was unfair, because he could not take any more garbage dumped on him.

He later reported a dream of dredging for gold, a situation I inferred as an example of the ideals he pursued, reminiscent of his early relation with his mother. Along with that was a heroic adherence to prison psychology, reflective of his long years of institutionalization. That psychology was exemplified in the next hour by revelation of his theft of coffee from the nursing station, and a fantasy of kidnap of a celebrity. He linked it to his boredom. He realized the audacity of such stealing, and its autistic nature.

He presented a multitude of dreams, of the Vietnam War, a Jeckle-Hyde scare of a pretty girl, slitting of a man's throat over coffee. I noted the power of his mind. He realized the competition he had with his friend, Phillips, for attainment of reality, and leaving the hospital. He was becoming sober about his heroics. He dreamed about cutoff arms and legs, a woman who fled, and my death, followed by that of a patient the unit was mourning. He realized the emptiness of his heroics and hypomanic dreams. He dreamt of a basic change of Patrick's manic grin, and also made contact with himself as a normal kid.

In the next hour he despaired of ever leaving the hospital, the impossibility of controlling his temper, relating it to killing animals, an impulsion since age 12. He took to announcing that he had dreams for me. In one he has sex with a lesbian psychologist, prehensile spiders. In a state of intuitive connection with the patient, I experienced the patient kissing me. This was followed by his request that I transfer him to Patton State Hospital.

Four months after inception of individual treatment, Valliant expressed remorse about a dream of the death of his younger sister, due to his reckless driving. There was an exchange about what he took as my presumptuousness in criticizing God. Then he accepted my designation of him as a Don Juan, who serves and conquers women. The intuitive connection was significant at that point, again followed by an experience on my part that the patient kissed me. I acknowledged an emotional connection with the patient. His dreams turned to reconciliatory theses, culminating with admission of an identity with another patient's psychopathic and benign aspects. He then expressed guilt about his murder of the animals, associated to his mother's feeding of the family at odd hours, identified with her and her negative moods.

Valliant moved away from partnership, both in crime and recovery, with Phillips, and at the same time, felt alone and at bottom, or nadir. The nadir state was combined with intuitive connection with me, itself combined with a wish to return to his family, versus his former alienation. There were more thoughts of death, destruction, despair and panic states. He realized he is not used to a normal, responsible state. Freedom involved having the world on his shoulders.

Valliant was messianic about a fellow patient with cancer, also worshipped the ground his mother walked on. When she left, it tore his world apart. He was a mythic rescuer of women, and he experienced a profound reaction after he left the Relaxation-Meditation group, conducted by a female rehabilitation therapist. He dreamed of saying goodbye to his mother. He had her on a pedestal, and now saw her as fallible. He spoke of his sister's letter of reconciliation; of having to be best as a flaw of character. He had a memory of sitting on mother's lap, she singing. He transferred the dream to sleeping with a nurse, a nonsexual event, seeking specialness. He could not forgive himself for his crime; felt like a wild animal. His father's family was violent.

The patient was taking deep counsel with self, renegotiating his relationship with me, as well as himself. He was aware of his regression when he stopped condemning himself as bad, alien, resulting in internal stress. Then, he searched his soul for family genetics, finding evidence of his alienation on both sides of the family. He was normal at 15, though bad tempered. Patient was touching base with a state of living in reality, a state he occupied in mid-adolescence, and the alienation he experienced in others' eyes when he was shunned. Also remarkable was the repeated intuitive connectedness in this session. He reached for a normalizing hobby, a friendship.

Eight months after inception, he regressed in a positive manner from adherence to the original idealistic therapeutic alliance with me, moving back to a previous psychiatrist in the Idaho State Hospital system, illustrating his own unreliability. Then he switched to data about his crime, on its anniversary. That started with idealistic caring and nurturing. Reflecting his parents' bossiness, he would be bossy, forcing himself on the girl, to overcome his shyness and the handicap of foster child origins. Then he switched to the dynamic of his relations with his siblings, whom he ruled out of fear. The intuitive connection at that point indicated his awareness of the transference connection of a psychoanalytic sort. He then suffered anxiety, secondary to the renegotiation of his values, centering on faith. He then cried in the group therapy about doing 110% for her, in accordance with her idealism. He continued his self-change project, working himself into a useful regimen on a productive job, along with emancipation from an addiction to tobacco. He felt old and out of shape. Family members wrote to him in reconciliation. One brother was the person he might have been.

Valliant reported that his soul was at peace, though Corker goaded him about his betrayal of the prison code. He still experienced interior anxiety and panic, from the separation from former antisocial heroic ideal. Living down his nadir status, lacking the saving hero one, renders him liable to instability and despair. He was susceptible to hedonic aspects of feminine identity, experiencing women in a paranoid way. Also, paradoxically, his peers were sensitive to his yielding to prosocial ways. He furnished coffee gratis to a patient in the canteen, illustrative of his inability to say no. It was the least severe infraction of the rules, letting him be true to the antisocial code. In a symbolic gesture in that direction, he furnished free coffee to another patient, losing his advanced security status.

Ten months after inception of the therapy, Valliant took refuge in his messianic identity, his commitment to God, during this stressful period. I recommended pastoral psychotherapy, and transaction with a staff minister, Rev. David Dod, a forceful, kindly middle-aged man who lent himself to dialogue about and with God. A far ranging pastoral session reached its critical point when the patient cited his despair, his inability to take another step. He then cited his passionate hatred of AA and the Godhead. Rev. Dod replied to the issue of evasion of spiritual responsibility, and the nature of covenant. He could understand why, because of hurt and abuse, this would lead to alienation from self. Dod then quoted Jesus' care for the least among them, how dredging the deep for monsters engaged one in reconciliation, and the assumption of an in between Robin Hood role towards rescuing self. He then cited his compulsiveness in squeezing a blister until it burst, versus a natural way of handling it. A detailed account of the work with Rev. Dod and its pastoral implications is found in Chapter VI: Pastoral Collaboration, and further detail is given in Appendix B3.

Valliant then reported an auditory hallucination in the group, of his name being called (by God) with no one there. He then went on to cite his hatred of black music, stemming from his mother's affair with a black man. He then experienced violent retching, related to an internal object, oedipal in nature. It was through this process that he unburdened himself of a mélange of memories, in the context of a Job-like desire to cry. Central there was a loss of belief in his mother and God, guilty along with the rest of humanity. There was a strong intuitive connection. He was working through alien identifications and reconciliation, envisioning returning to the family, sans his specialness.

By 1995, Valliant had accepted the loss of his pedestal position, his here-and-now status. He was still trusting Jesus. He then visited the reality of his psychiatric history, the role of medication in dealing with his hyperactivity, perversity, and self-alienation after his mother's departure. Then came his baptism and spiritual crisis, working through the loss. He wondered if his mental ailments stemmed from her and her messianism, putting kids on a pedestal. He realized that he sought justice through violence, and began choking himself and crying for his mother, against injustice.

Interpersonal and intrapsychic change came in a rush. Valliant related that after he threw his Bible away, he suffered zombie status and the night of the living dead. Now he reconciled with his family. He cried over saying goodbye to the hospital, and was also still breaking his ties with the antisocial group. He revisited the rape scene, his domination through a bite of her breast. He finally broke from tobacco, which had been his God, and was also the Joseph of his family. He could not believe she gave them up. He dreamed of being buried alive in a coffin; had been claustrophobic since being in seclusion at age 7.

Valliant continued to feel the doctor and minister are out to find fault, to keep him here forever. He identified with an intrusive, assaultive patient. He was trapped within himself, enraged, still working within his self. His soul was black; with a large hole in self. In this seminal session, Valliant reached to his soul, his alienated identity, and at the same time, identified with another alienated peer. He continued in part schizophrenese, part earnest revelatory manner, to explore his evil identity.

He was edged into remorse about impregnating a woman. He reported success in avoiding a temper outburst this morning. Reconciling with his ideal for himself; he had his best sleep ever. He could see the value of choice over paranoid tendency; was able to see how he lost himself to his compulsions.

By late 1995, Valliant reported he no longer had an explosive temper; he had a soul of his own. He was creating a myth of alienation and redemption, leading Rev. Dod to ask if he has magically conjured it up. He was also redefining himself with his fellows. He was making amends with the animals, through poetry. He realized he had regressed to God status. He reported a dream of being buried alive in a pine box; when he woke up, he had a fear of suffocation. He was accepting the ambiguity and disorder of reality.

A year and a half after inception, he identified a change, with God back in his life, upon commitment by the rehabilitation therapist to work with him. There was her subsequent authentic rage, and his subsequent Pruno episode in which he secretly made a fruit liquor. He worked with a nurse on his crime through a decision matrix. He took a respite from analysis to be "normal, human." Earlier in life, he had been compulsively good, and belonged to it. He linked his sensitivity to manic states in others and self with his tie to his mother and seeing her as a separate person, demythologized. He discussed the issue of his mother's possible fear of him, versus his protective stance; and his rage at his Dad.

Valliant experienced emotional agony, relative to the separation, when his brother sent a package. He reported being in a haunted state since childhood, like Casper and the ghost. Then he reported feeling confident, dependable on his job. I noted improvement, a closeness with fellow patients. He opened up in an AA group about killing animals, and was mothered by the members.

During his final session before leaving Ash, Valliant expressed painful and happy emotions, crying about leaving ASH, his home for 14 years. The session centered on integrity and his awareness of his family's pathology of overdoing it. He was still agonized by the loss of his father, who failed the family. He was the ideal figure to his mother.

Valliant is acting normal in the Trailer Project, striving with might and main to alter his character towards normalcy. He has anger at his loss of individuality in having to reach out to others, and is also in a self-persecutory role.

Valliant completed his substance-abuse course, demonstrated efficiency at work at the canteen, and completed a 12-step program. He had been a participant in group and individual therapies in a productive manner, displaying increasing accessibility and participation. In a representative report at this time, he stated his intention was to continue his work on his problems. He was in the 12-step program trekking through his past vicious animal-murdering tendencies. He was also noted to be working with the author and the chaplain, to guide him on his spiritual concerns in a productive manner. He continued to be outgoing and participative in groups. There were no extrapyramidal symptoms or unusual movements. He was continued on Sertraline and Depakote. Since then, he worked in the Trailer Project, productively. In all, Valliant made slow but definite progress. The treatment team considered that he could continue progress at Napa State Hospital.

Commentary (from notes made upon Valliant's last day at ASH)

On termination of his treatment, this patient remains a work in progress, but the progress is discernible. His explosive temper is gone, his demeanor is changed from a "wise Gorber grin" to that of a relatively calm student. He applies himself to productive pursuits, in this case a job in the canteen. He still is a leader of his fellows, but it is prosocial. His internal life has been markedly altered from its paranoid, psychopathic cast, in which he had a malign ego ideal to one that is messianic in cast, given to scruples. His dream life, earlier tending to deeply morbid scenarios, is more mundane and problem-solving. Intuitive connection occurs in most of his sessions. Again, the reader is urged to access the detailed account in Appendix B3. I have presented work on the material on Wards 10 and 24 sufficient in detail to perhaps whet the appetite of the reader for further study. As elsewhere in my career, through the therapeutic community method I was able to mobilize the patient toward self-care. This was done sufficiently so they could leave their alienated worlds and collaborate with me and the personnel in rejoining reality. Success there led to collaboration elsewhere in institutional self-change as in work with the families, the managerial revolution of Continuous Quality Improvement, and staff reeducation.

Summary

On review of the thirty-nine pages of this chapter, with its many characters, their disparate life circumstances, and their interior lives consisting of death, destruction, resurrection, and restitution, two words stand out: alienation and reconciliation. The members were profoundly alienated from themselves and becoming reconciled through their life together, that with the devoted personnel, and with me acting as an agent who had learned his trade and profession in a search for my very soul. It was on that basis that I transacted with the patient Jones on Ward Ten at the inception of the Therapeutic Community, and on that basis that he responded and left his antisocial identity. We then supported him in his newfound role and capacity as a co-leader of our democratic enterprise. He and his fellows then shared truths about their situation, and one truth was that of hope. The Living In Reality group shared a manly commitment in that direction, as did its members in braving the work with me in that strange exercise in ambiguity that was psychoanalytic therapy.

As this exercise progressed, fragments of personality revivified, coalesced, and normal appetites for living took hold. Horseplay became rare. As an example, Valliant found himself a job, quit nicotine, and planned for his future. Sucras applied his now-keen intelligence to the CAT test. The death we had encountered at inception of these thirty-nine patients had given way to renewed life.

CHAPTER III

Institutional Self-Transformation: Treatment Improvement Project, Quality Circle Movement, and Therapeutic Community

The Treatment Improvement Project Breaks Ground

The hospital was engaged at the time in what was called quality assurance, in which inspection was the mode of monitoring and intervention. In treatment improvement, *management* called on staff to initiate fundamental change. Clyde L. Murray, the Deputy Director of the Department of Mental Health in a Draft Special Order called for a survey by the hospitals of a core set of treatment activities, monitored for effectiveness. He emphasized collaborative and informed relationships with the patients in which they would be educated about their illness and participate in their treatment. Dr. Mayer, the Director of the Department, met with the staff of Atascadero State Hospital in mid-1991 in a town hall format to emphasize support for the new venture. The new Executive Director of ASH called for treatment improvement, and a Clinical Management Team began the process of assessing present treatment.

A Facility Steering Committee was appointed to develop a comprehensive plan to improve treatment within present resources. Dr. Robert Behan, Acting Chief of Staff, assembled an *ad hoc* Committee for the Development of a Coordinated Treatment Program. It held a workshop on psychosocial rehabilitation by Dr. Robert Hierhozer.

In two months of meetings, it inquired into the roles of the disciplines in treatment and psychosocial rehabilitation. They rendered a report and plan for implementation to the Facility Treatment Improvement Project Steering Committee. The concept of the bio-psychosocial rehabilitation model was to be used to maximize treatment effectiveness. The focus was to be an enhanced recognition of where the patients were going and what barriers to their ultimate placement could be identified. These barriers were often the result of a lack of specific coping skills required within the treatment setting. The committee's goal was not to develop a cookbook process but to develop a self-correcting system for treatment delivery.

The steering committee met regularly beginning in early May. Soon after its inception, Dr. Behan appointed me as its Acting Chair. It conducted an assessment of the organizational realities, historical structures and basic assumptions that serve as the environment in which we were presently providing services. This process resulted in a clear need to restructure the patient placement/treatment delivery system along the lines which have as their focus this positional outcome as the prime determinant.

The committee completed its task with the following assumptions:

1. Fundamental treatment modalities such as pharmacology, longer range detoxification, medical diagnosis and stability stabilization, and appropriate nutrition, continued to be foremost.
2. Psychosocial rehabilitation was an organized system by which social behaviors and skills could be taught and attained in order to expand and strengthen capacity.
3. Learning via the PSR model took a variety of forms, but it was objective by pre-imposed measurements and it was ultimately validated by successful positional placement.

The Birth of the CQI Movement

CQI was begun by the management guru Edwards Deming, whose quality circle methodology transformed postwar Japanese industry. All the participants in the productive process conferred in equity to shape the product or service. Therapeutic community had similar philosophy and practice, involving collaboration of the members of the community in changing itself for optimal productivity. It assembled patients and personnel to identify and solve the problems which arise. One stemmed from industry, the other medicine, and their competition and collaboration make up the story of this piece on institutional change at Atascadero State Hospital.

Continuous quality improvement has an analogous basic procedure, seeking correction of defect in the productive process through the collaboration of the entire range of producers and distributors. Towards that end, a new profession of management consultant was born, and the formation of quality circles, a group formation that has had a history of its own. That history can be traced back to the Middle Ages, and efforts by the Guilds to control quality by inspection. With the onset of the industrial age, inspection was the prime method of control of quality. Karl Marx, in *Das Kapital*, identified the problem in production as the alienation of the productive agent, the worker from the fact of gain, and the value added by the organizer of the productive process, or capitalist. In 1911, Frederick W. Taylor published *The Principles of Scientific Management*, providing a framework for effective utilization of people in production. He emphasized clearly defined tasks under standard conditions. Inspection to prevent defect from leaving the factory was a central tenet, performed at the end of the process, and the formation of a quality control department led to the concept of quality control.

Statistical theory made an appearance with the publication in the 1920s by Dr. W. Showhart of the first modern control chart, demonstrating that variation in production led to variation in product. The next intervention into the productive process was in the 1940s at the General Electric plants in New York and Western Electric at the Hawthorne Works, Illinois. In the '40s, the psychologist Abraham Maslow wrote on self-actualization and meaningful job responsibility. The enormous expansion of the arms industry in World War II entailed efforts to control quality through inspection. W. Edwards Deming, an American engineer, pioneered a method of quality control that was first rejected by American companies, but bought by Japanese industry after World War II. It eventuated into the profession of quality control, its chief practitioners being W. Edwards Deming, Joseph Juran, and Philip B. Crosby. Juran introduced the concept and practice of quality circles in 1967. Deming returned from Japan in the 1970s to spread the word to American industry. By 1982, an estimated 1,500 American public and private organizations had team problem-solving programs.

The three gurus evolved different methods. On top of that, their proving ground, Japan, created an efflorescence of methodologies and a literature to match. Deming as inspirational authority worked from the top down, emphasizing statistics. Juran worked bottom up, supplying ways to search out and process data. Crosby emphasized motivation and follow-through. But the message of all three gurus was commitment to quality improvement throughout the organization as the ultimate tool. One attacked the system rather than the employee. One stripped down the work process to find and eliminate problems that prevent quality. Identify the customer, internal and external, to satisfy requirements in the work process or finished product. Eliminate waste, instill pride and teamwork, and create an atmosphere of innovation for continued and permanent quality improvement.

CQI at ASH

In 1992, the Joint Commission on Accreditation of Healthcare Organizations in its 1992 edition of the *Accreditation Manual for Hospitals* revised its quality assurance chapter to incorporate CQI concepts. It noted that the benefits of CQI could not be realized in response to the requirements of an external agency, but could evolve from an internal commitment to organizational change that took place over a number of years. In 1992, JCAHO required all hospital leaders to receive CQI training. CQI was to be implemented the following year.

A year before, in 1991, ASH searched for CQI training, settling in Spring 1992 on Organizational Dynamics as the training agency. In Spring 1992, hospital leaders had their first training, two seminars. In June 1992, forty staff members received basic training. Twenty received more advanced training, Quality Advantage Training, and were designated as trainers. Twenty others received Quality Action Team training, and were designated as facilitators. In September 1992, The Quality Council and Quality Improvement Team received training. In October, a total of 76 people were trained, and in November, 60 more.

CQI Versus QA

Continuous Quality Improvement was compared with Quality Assurance, its previous improvement intervention. CQI looked at the various processes and the system that affected performance and outcome. QA looked at the individual or department performance, or at people. CQI reviewed interdepartmental processes, versus isolated departmental activities. CQI openly acknowledged the contribution of support services to the overall outcome, could be applied to any process, and looked to integrate or coordinate duplication of effort and reduce the potential for error, versus focus on the clinical areas only. CQI was non-punitive, educational. CQI involved all employees, encouraged team building across disciplines and services, versus reliance on a single QA program to ensure quality. CQI was an ongoing process versus focus on identifying problems. CQI was based on prevention, versus inspection. CQI principles could be incorporated into QA, except for a different focus and approach, when QA provided a place from which CQI could evolve.

CQI was based on two management systems studied and developed over the past forty years, Participatory Management and Statistical Quality Control. The former eschewed punishment and reward, made work more meaningful, encouraged worker participation and responsibility, and gave the people closest to the problems the responsibility, training, and support necessary to solve them.

Quality Circles

Quality circles were groups of employees who voluntarily met together on a regular basis to identify, define, analyze and solve work related problems. Usually, the members of a particular team quality circle were from the same work area, all of whom do similar work, so that the problems they selected were familiar to all of them. In addition, inter-departmental or cross-functional quality circles could also be formed. An ideal size of quality circle was 7 to 8 members, but the number of members in a quality circle could vary. There were alternate names for quality circles: small groups, action circles, excellence search tools, human resources circles, productivity circles.

Objectives of quality circles: promote job involvement, create prob-lem-solving capability, improve communication, promote leadership qualities, promote personal development, develop greater awareness, develop greater awareness for safety, improve morale through closer identity of employee objectives with organization's objectives, reduce errors, enhance quality, inspire more effective teamwork, build an atti-tude of problem prevention, promote cost reduction, develop harmoni-ous manager, supervisor and worker relationship, improve productivity, reduce downtime for machines and equipment, increase employee motivation.

Quality circle meetings were an important part of the work, attended by all the members of the quality circle, in general once a week or fort-night, lasting approximately one hour, seeking regularity of meeting. The activity during the meeting could have been cited as: identifying a theme or a problem to work on, getting training required to enable members to analyze problems, analyzing problems, preparing recom-mendations for implementation, follow-up, preparation of presentation to the management.

Misconception concerning quality circles: they did not tackle just quality problems, they did not substitute for task forces, product committees, joint plant councils or work committees, quality assurance departments, suggestion schemes. They did not change the existing organizational structure or chain of command. They were not a forum for grievances or a springboard for demands. They were not a means for the management to unload all their problems. They were not just another technique, or a panacea for all ills.

Pitfalls and problems could be cited as: lack of faith in and support to quality circle activities among management personnel, lack of interest or income, apathy, fear and misunderstanding among middle level executives, pretense of leader/facilitators, delay or non-implementation of circle recommendations, irregularity of quality circle activities, non-application of simple techniques for problem solving, lack of or non-participation by some members in the circle activities, circles running out of problems, antagonism of nonmembers towards quality circle operations, inadequate visibility of management support, complexity of problems taken up, non-maintenance of quality circle records, too much facilitation/too little communication/communication gaps between circles and departmental head, change of management, confusing quality circle for another technique, and resistance from trade unions.

Code of conduct for quality circles: attend all meetings and be on time. Listen to, and show respect for the views of other members, make others feel a part of the group, criticize ideas, not persons, help other members to participate more fully, be open to and encourage the ideas of others. Every member is responsible for the team's progress, maintain a friendly attitude, strive for enthusiasm, the only stupid question is the one that is not asked, look for marriage in the ideas of others, pay attention and avoid disruptive behavior, avoid actions that delay progress, carry out assignments on schedule, give credit to those to whom it is due, thank those who give assistance, do not suppress ideas but express them, objectives and causes first, solutions next, ideas generated by the group.

Quality circle tools: brainstorming, Pareto analysis, cause and effect diagram, fishbone or Ishikawa, histogram, scatter diagram, stratification, check sheet, control charts and graphs, relations diagram, affinity diagram, systematic or tree diagram, matrix diagram, makeshift data analysis diagram, process decision program chart, arrow diagram.

Benefits of quality circles: self-development, promotes leadership qualities among participants, recognition, achievement satisfaction, promotes group/team working, serves as cementing force between management and other groups, promotes continuous improvement in products and services, brings about a change in environment of more productivity, better quality, reduces costs, safety and corresponding rewards.

CQI generated the tools to aid the individual and his group to solve problems at work, enlisting collaboration of management. Management ceased to depend on inspection, but is exposed to data all the way to the grassroots of the system. A state of mutual confidence, versus macho management, is attained and maintained throughout, and repaired when impaired.

Systematic CQI Training at ASH

The training at ASH started with the executives at the top, and proceeded until all management and half of the clinical staff were trained. Having established a Quality Council, the working party proceeded to survey for problem areas. The clinical chart distribution system, feeding of the patients, patient violence, and adverse drug reactions were deemed suitable for initial inquiry.

The centerpiece of the training was the acronym FADE, standing for Focus, Analyze, Develop and Execute. This tool is evidently a guide to critical examination of data, sorting them, adducing meaning, and appropriate action.

The practitioner of CQI is called a facilitator. Like the psychoanalytic counterpart in mental health, a facilitator does not solve the problem, but enables the perplexed individual or group to solve it. The facilitator employs a specific professional approach, fortified by a number of tools, techniques and exercises which helps the group to assemble, sort, analyze, integrate, and synthesize information.

It took a full week of intensive meetings to begin to get the gist of what was required, to learn and use the tools, then to practice the role of facilitator. In the process, our personalities and, at times, our very souls were stretched. Hospital administration selected 20 of us, representing psychiatry, psychology, social work, administration, dietary service, security, rehabilitation, patient rights, nursing, and level of care. Many of us knew only a few in the group. At first, conscious of our and the other's position in ASH's hierarchy, we achieved a remarkable level of equity and mutuality.

We sat in a U formation, facing the instructor. He introduced himself, his background from business and that of the quality movement, and what he intended to do with us. He had us introduce ourselves, going the rounds. He began telling of the quality action teams with whom we were to consult. He cited the slogan, "You are my customers. I need to know what your needs are. You are to learn here enough to be dangerous." Knowing that we have danger enough at ASH and that our administration must have good reason to trust its hospital to continuous quality and our group of 20 fledgling facilitators, we proceeded with what turned out to be 2 1/2 days of assimilating material, and another 2 1/2 days of practice.

He gave an overview of the problem-solving process called FADE, the structured process of Focus, Analyze, Develop, and Execute. In Focus, one chose a problem and described it. In Analyze, one learned about the problem from data. In Develop, one developed a solution and a plan. In Execute, one implemented the plan, monitored results, and adjusted as needed.

Under his direction, we formed ourselves into four teams, consisting of the members who sat next to each other. Whoever assigned our places did a good job, because we got along exceedingly well. In fact, the group as a whole became quite convivial and collegial. We were as supportive as a good therapy group, stayed very well in reality, and took into constructive account pertinent underlying personal factors. Humor was a marvelous lubricant to make the days, packed with lessons, slide by.

The subject these teams took up first must have had a great deal with why we formed an alliance so quickly. In therapy we call this alliance the therapeutic alliance. A similar bonding is still often absent in education. It is my observation that without such bonding, the most masterfully done quality improvement techniques will be in vain.

We were asked to be up front in our individual hopes and fears regarding quality improvement. We were then asked to work out team formations of those concerns. We had reported such to the plenary group. As in encounter and therapy group work, the members' emotions were mobilized and it turned into a moving, if not poignant experience.

I believe that is when we became bonded into a group, committed to the enterprise, even though the question of what quality improvement really was "slid through our fingers." Members, committed to the enterprise, were afraid employees would tend to kill the messenger. However, we voiced interest in interaction with various parts of the hospital, especially those who worked directly with the patients.

We then set out ground rules and a code of behavior. We agreed with our mentor to support each other's opinions, not put each other down, engage in conflict in a constructive manner, to keep it simple, and leave the bars and stars at the door. Lastly, we agreed to have fun.

We then spent some time on who were our customers—the patients, courts, or employees. We saw that we would have to envision them all for what they were, as human entities, in serving them. We would have avoided the chief administrative pitfall, of filtering initiative and data down from the top. We needed to reach out to the programs and units systematically. We needed to keep in mind that we ultimately had to please the outside community, which we safeguard.

We were exposed to the first of what turned out to be 23 tools. A tool is a structured, conducted way for the individual or group to pursue solving problems, based on the experience of one of the most prominent of the companies in the quality improvement field. In demonstrating our first tool, our mentor, drawing on a flipchart, erected five pediments supporting a pyramid on a base of values. The pediments were labeled Patient Focus, Total Involvement, Measurement, Systematic Support, and Continuous Improvement. They each were necessary for the structure to stand.

The next tool was egg shaped, with four quadrants, labeled Execute, and Focus in the upper quadrants, and Develop and Analyze in the lower. These are the steps, starting with Focus, moving to Analyze, then Develop, then finally Execute.

Next came the "Quality Grid." It related to basic considerations on striving for perfection. It was a square, with an arrow labeled "How" above, and "What" on its right hand side. It was divided into four boxes, labeled on top R T W (Right Things Wrong), RTR (Right Things Right), and on bottom, WTW (Wrong Things Wrong), and WTR (Wrong Things Right). The purpose was to show the vectors of motivations and methods and approach to quality, which is doing Right Things Right. (Also, it trained one not to get too excited when one thinks wrong, a step to professionalism). Again, it was important to "do things right rather than do the right thing." He gave us examples of doing "Wrong Things Wrong," the new Coke, the Edsel, and the Gulf War. He gave as "Right Things Wrong" the disasters of Bhopal, the Exxon Valdez, Chernobyl, and the Challenger. He asked for members to furnish and categorize a major task they performed in the past two weeks. They did so with relish.

He commented that it was a question of the work environment, and our limited control. He stated baldly that *94% of the problems relate to process*, by which he meant this system in which people are enmeshed; 6% is due to the people themselves. Most employees want to do what is right. People are generally dictatorial because they are insecure. Of those, 6% are up front. Mostly there is a curtain over those processes. He likened the phenomenon to a vacuum filled with a negative valence.

In continuous quality, we guide a relatively autonomous group as it feels and thinks through strategy to deal with problem areas. He cited that the more one gets to know the individual behind the process, the more the negative is worked through. Members of the group commented that, generally, the process at ASH expects the minimum of employees. Another stated that S.S.I. could save the enormous expense of the evaluation by rewarding all who applied for funds.

At that point, our mentor asked members to relate in one word what went on in their heads concerning continuous quality. They answered: impatient, ruminative, headache, confused, cautious, fuzzy, anticipative, late, uncertain, anxious, worried, gratified (which was my association, for having opened up early about a complaint), overwhelmed, sleepy, and waiting. Members sought to elaborate: What does that mean? Why is it there? We are working up to it. We bounced the subject of meaning about like a good therapy group as the guided associations became freer. Those skeptical in the group joined in, to the effect that they had been through it, and hoped that it was different this time.

Our mentor asked us if we knew what was expected of us. Members related that they had heard they were to put in 4 to 8 hours per week, for 18 months, "facilitating." They asked its relationship to quality assurance and to the quality advantage of next week. There was some discussion of the relationship of "mahogany row" to the profound changes continuous quality brings to organizations, taking years to show.

We were then asked to brainstorm the qualities and role of a team leader, and of a trainer-facilitator. We came up with: s/he elicits trust, believes in the team, helps stay in focus, has good communication skills, has vision, sees the big picture, is enthusiastic, courageous, draws members in, is a catalyst, a model, gatekeeper, funnels ideas, enhances, summarizes, synthesizes; is objective, motivates, facilitates, and arbitrates.

He turned us next to managing time, focused on that which gets in the way. He sent us to brainstorming factors in choosing a vacation site, by means of a Selection Grid. He listed the destinations vertically, and the Cost, Transit Time, Activity, and Climate Management Problems horizontally.

He then turned us to Impact Analysis, a very important tool to determine if a problem is worth working on, its extent, and the differing viewpoints of the group concerning it. He elicited designations for negative impact: demoralizing, losing good people, extra work, "sneaky ways," the needs may not exist, extra stress, excessive cost, and overtime work.

He next came to the Problem Statement, a technique for describing a problem, its impact, and the desired state. Another important tool, it is used for gaining consensus, explaining to someone outside the team what the problem is, and demonstrating the effects of the problem and the benefits of solving it. A flip chart page is divided into three horizontal sections: Current State, Impact, and Desired State. One concisely fills in the boxes using the brainstorming method. One can fill in the impact of correcting the problem. Agreement of the team members is sought, of course.

The person in the organization and team who is most resistant may have the key to the problem. Another unorthodox approach is "solution jumping," in which one backs up on the expected method, intuitively. Another is Innovation Transfer, in which, when one feels blocked in the process, one innovatively sets up a different problem, the feelings and factors associated with it, sets them forth in their problem statement, then sets forth the Past Statement alongside the Current Situation. The fit will not be exact in all cases, but the comparisons are calculated to *open the minds of the participants.*

In line with this free-flowing way of going, members opened up about their concerns of the moment. We discussed the relation of the team leader to the facilitator. The leader is responsible for implementation. The facilitator got the process going. The facilitator trains team leaders. People are not comfortable with the new management style of bringing employees into the process. In changing the traditional way of going, one takes initiative, while clearing with somebody, and following the manual at the same time.

Trainees brought up their problems with current work overload and a lack of time, the current rigid committee and administrative director structure, and the fact that the current hospital culture discourages intrusion of new ideas. We do not have any way of measuring whether and how the patient is taken care of, measurement of our output. On the other hand, we know when there are no scandals.

The attention of the group turned to tracking changes in leadership on various levels, with a special task of the Executive Director indicating support of CQI from the first, in action as well as word. The members acknowledged the need for control at ASH, but also the imperative to get the employee involved in decision-making. You own the problem until it is solved, whatever levels of administration and practice are involved.

Our mentor then took up the Analyze phase of FADE. One decides what one needs to know, identifies patterns, collects baseline data, and determines influential factors. One attends to processes, rather than people. One makes darn sure it is not the process, and one shoots throughout for the root cause. I might add that one keeps intuitive processes to the fore throughout the FADE experience.

Our mentor stated that one mobilizes the cognitive synergy of the group. He gave as an example: the processes one goes through in planning a party. Utilizing post-it notes he laid up the key operations for planning a party, such as location, date, time, guest list, wine, food, etc. We would then do a flowchart. The group became aware of its capacity for "being on the ball," its cognitive capacity.

There was a schema behind the data-gathering: there was a focus, a sense of when there were no data, their accuracy, relevance, timeliness, and alternates sources. A dry run was useful to "tune up" cognitive processes. Sampling and survey are types of data-gathering. One can sample randomly in subsets or strata, or systematically. Next comes the assumption or hypothesis to be tested and the nature of the population of the governing factors. Collection and assessment go hand-in-hand. A check-sheet is useful, utilizing a bar graph of items on the horizontal, and quantity on the vertical.

Our mentor then drew the Fishbone Diagram, one of the most useful tools in purposeful data collection. On the left he drew two large vertical V's, connected at their points by a line, the spine of the fish, pointed at them leading to a succinct designation of the problem.

In this instance, it was the Causes of Marital Arguments. The top fish ribs were severally labeled People and Materials, the bottom Machines and Methods. We started filling in the categories of possible causative factors, children and stepchildren, in-laws for People, money for Materials, autos for Machines, and cultural values and job responsibility for Methods. We did a Pareto Diagram or bar graph, assigning quantities to the items, to see which item we needed to focus on first.

We then readily did a Flow Chart of activity from awakening to arrival at work. This was followed by an interesting tool called Innovation Transfer, which is designed to open up the cognitive processes of the group which finds itself "stuck." The situation our mentor posed was a difficult sail, opened up by brainstorming a difficult "sail." The factors of a Difficult Sail were listed vertically: reduce sail, life jacket, owner's manual, batten down, safe ports, radio for assistance, sea anchor. Then he asked for the group's association to each item: reduced pressure, reduced price, improved terms, break, talk with salespeople, called boss, get to know client. A Fishbone Diagram could be used for the same purpose.

He then took up a long-term friend of industry, the Cost-Benefits Analysis. We compared costs of being an employee in differently organized companies, one in Florida, the other in Minnesota. We brainstormed cost factors, for the Florida location, such as swimming pool, air conditioning, pest control, weather maintenance, crime factor, transportation to school. We then did the benefits, such as less clothing, decreased school transportation cost, lower medical and fitness cost, lower education cost. We worked out a ratio of cost to benefit, making the Florida location more desirable, despite cultural advantages in Minnesota.

We then did a Force Field Analysis, which consists of listing and comparing factors driving the venture, versus those restraining it. ASH's continuous quality venture was used to illustrate. Factors driving were the joint commission, State Sen. Alquist, and the budget. Restraining factors were attitudes, apathy, laziness, California, rigidity of the system, budget, and politics. We then did a checklist for a successful date. The group came up with: bring wallets, don't be late, be clean, get recommendation, other couple you enjoy, blood tests. In association to that, we did one of the most important tools, the Contingency Diagram, on How To Have An Unsuccessful Date. He drew an hour on the left side of the flipchart, with lines radiating outwards. We brainstormed the factors code: be late, too aggressive, leave while others home, ignore, burp, no interesting comment, smell, scratch, wrong version, and passive-aggressive.

We took up SOP, or Standards Operating Procedure, brainstorming the steps. As illustration, he chose the micro staff steps in striking a match. SOP resembles a Flow Chart, but is more systematized. It is related to the more complicated Action Plan in which one lists What Needs To Be Done, Time To Be Completed, and Person Responsible.

We finally got to the Execution Phase. There the job was to gain Commitment, Execute, then Monitor the Impact. Measurement to Monitor followed. Multi-voting is a former measurement used in the FADE process, to ascertain the sentiment of team members for items they have previously brainstormed. They get 5 to 10 points to divide in place for items under scrutiny. Measurement is used to monitor a work process, gathering data to understand a problem, to identify unwanted variation at the start of a problem-solving cycle and complete it. In Building Individual Support, we were instructed to use the tool in which we, on a horizontal, listed What, Who, When, How To Get To, Person. In Developing Measures, one needed to Focus On The Problem, KISS (keep it simple stupid), be Action Oriented, attend to Action Results, attend to Customer, and also to Self.

A Measures Matrix was helpful in attending to self, versus the customer, in a car repair shop. Boxes on a flipchart were assigned to Self and Customer. Above them were listed Process and Results. The Self's process items were work order, invoices, parts, phone calls; results were jobs done, paid profit, and customer satisfaction. The Customers Process had: phone, confirm, and estimate; results there were: car fixed, and value. Another measures method illustrated was a line graph illustrating the Bell Curve of defective automobile doors, and its use in quality improvement.

We then practiced on another Contingency Diagram, on how to have an unsuccessful meeting: flaky schedule, late agenda, no minutes, late start, late and unsatisfactory meeting, and inappropriate team members. From that, we work out ways of having a successful meeting: a well-organized, motivated chairperson, solid agenda, meetings when appropriate, timelines of agenda and minutes, appropriate and motivated members, appropriate place, and involvement of the group in problem-solving.

We then had another of our communicative interludes, in which we exchanged concerning the role of the facilitator in rather direct manner. As professionals, we are bound by confidentiality, but to be reasonable about it, in terms of the organizational needs. We need to be honest, attempting to change the system or process, and not "hung up" on the difficulties of persons in the system, except in a facilitative manner. One needs to be able to take risks, first looking at the process. If it is a problem of the process, fix it: if not, fix the person; if you can't, take another action. Trust the group, and its process.

He proceeded to draw three concentric circles. The outer was labeled Panic; next, Learning; innermost, Comfort. He drew an arrow line from Comfort to outside the circles, labeling it Tension. He stated that 25% of people in any one meeting were with the facilitator, 10% were against, hostile and concerned, and 65% were engaging in some sort of sexual fantasy! The role of the facilitator is to manage the tension.

He then drew a chart of the Symptoms and Cure, relating to the circles of Comfort, Learning, and Panic. Under Comfort, he drew out of us the factors of: snore, side conversation, yawns, leaving, eyes drifting, and doodling. Under Cure for that, we came up with: exercise, questions, break, ask them, pull back, off-focus jokes, and what's going on? Under Learning Symptoms: questions relevant, eye contact, interaction, and association. Under Cure for Learning symptoms: keep doing it, reinforce, expand ideas, and break. Under Panic Symptoms: distracted, avoidance, arguments, and venting. Under Cure of Panic Symptoms: communication, acknowledge, positive information, support, get out of the way, and break.

Our mentor then sought leadership queries from the group, readily obtaining: where do we go from here? How is this useful? How does this impact you? How are you doing? I am sensing, and am I right? What are some of the things you tried? Who, what, when, and why? How does this apply? What comes to your mind? Are you with me? Where are you? All this carried us to that halfway mark in our course. We would then set the practice, each assigned a topic, the group acting as the team. After each presentation, lasting 20 minutes, the presenter, with feedback from the group and mentor, listed What Worked and What Would Be Done Differently. The presenter was requested to say "Thank you" to each feedback! The group was instructed to give a standing ovation, KISS (keep it simple stupid), keep it honest, and to be specific.

The group process was extremely successful, in that we became very spontaneous, yet very supportive and collegial in the best sense. We were direct and honest, and in a politic way. There was a great deal of opening up of presumptive use clique formations, boding well for change in the rigid structures of the hospital. It is of utmost importance that the facilitator group meet regularly for continued growth of its hard-won skills. At this point in our development, before they are fixed in certainty, we can expect to lose them quickly. With them will go our new found professional identity and usefulness to the hospital as we slip back into our jobs.

Use of this method, which is more than a collection of tools, will help us to change the way we operate the hospital and deal with one another. Its use will also be crucial in helping us restructure the hospital when the cuts in services come about. All this is bound to be of value to our patients, a happier, more efficient staff changing for the better.

However, the real test lies in the help quality improvement afforded the treatment improvement project to come online shortly. To that end, I proposed three initiatives, which could and should be subjected to quality improvement scrutiny: a professional form, hospital-wide work-shop based on the treatment team, and a group work training program that are aimed to bring the professions closer to work on problems, and lend themselves to the quality improvement approach. Copies were available at the medical staff office.

There must be facility plan level proposals, springing from the grass-roots that can change capital ASH for the better. Quality improvement calls for open dialogue openly arrived at. It is in the spirit of that dialogue I presented this piece to be brainstormed and added to by fellow facilitators and debated by the hospital staff. 4 September 1992, Chair, Department of Psychiatry.

Training of the Quality Council

The problem I chose in the course of my training was the cost and mor-bidity associated with smoking at ASH, and centered my exercise on a tool called force field analysis. Through the process of brainstorming, the group quickly assembled on the flipchart a list of the forces driving ASH's population, patient and personnel, towards a smoke-free environment, and those restraining it, keeping smoking going. We listed them in adjacent columns labeled Driving and Restraining. We collaborated in formulating the language used to table the factors. When we ran dry, we set to stating possible solutions. Examining and discussing the flipchart, it became readily apparent to us what would happen to the social equation. ASH would move towards a smoke-free environment.

Moreover, the logic of the FADE tools began to dawn on us. Looking at the diagram, we could see that an action plan could be easily derived from the force field tool, as well as the tools of impact analysis, flowchart, and standard operating procedure. In our minds, we began implementation of the action plan, and so entered the execute phase. We turned to tools for measuring and monitoring. Measuring was appropriate to earlier steps in that FADE cycle, including the formulation of the action plan. It was especially needed in monitoring the impact of implementation. We quickly moved through the tools of bar graph, pie chart, and line graph. We examined the application of control limits to a line graph, the measurement tool most useful in monitoring the course of smoking cessation. Through it one can tell a complex situation at a glance. It was interesting that in the course of the free exchanges on the smoking situation, data emerged on the course of caffeine restriction. We also discussed social science monitoring through historical techniques and documentaries. We had come to the end of the day, exhausted yet quite stimulated by our efforts. If the past training experience of the facilitators is any guide, I would expect that the appetite of the participants in this venture for more training would be whetted.

They will be playing a central role in ASH's application of the quality improvement discipline to solve deep-seated problems.

The quality improvement method seeks nothing less than transformation of an institution's way of going. The Quality Council and Quality Improvement Team have launched themselves on this ambitious voyage. 5 September, 1992.

In the Midst of Change: ASH, TIP, and CQI

We at ASH have begun a momentous effort at simultaneously changing how we engage in the exercise in human problem-solving that is therapy (TIP), and the way we manage that process (CQI). So far, it has been a source of considerable interest, but mounting stress. Without a state of mutual confidence as we proceeded through this journey, we placed our forensic enterprise and ourselves in some danger. With it, success was assured. This essay, written at that time, was devoted to that state of mutuality. I intended to sketch the forest and the trees, what I considered to be core meanings in this massive, complex venture, where I thought we were going, what we could expect to go through, pitfalls along the way, and possible ways to avoid them.

We started preparation in 1990, and were in the midst of the treatment improvement projects, massive shifts of patients and personnel. There we aimed towards alignment to a more purposeful, outcome-oriented treatment, and employment of the elements of psychosocial rehabilitation appropriate to our forensic population.

A year after initiating development of TIP, we began training in continuous quality improvement, to change our "culture," of solving problems in the productive process of patient recovery that constitutes treatment. It would have been desirable to have first mastered CQI, so we could have the advantage of its quality circle method. There the people and units we have been moving would have participated in working out its rationale and mechanics. It is highly likely that ASH would have experienced a great mobilization of initiative and participation. If our experience with CQI so far is any guide, we would have enjoyed it, in marked contrast to what is still an extremely stressful experience.

In the quality method, productive groups, called quality circles, take on relatively autonomous function, in partnership with management. Together, they bend their efforts towards solution of agreed on problems. In CQI, no one is a passive agent, all have an equal voice in the phases of problem-solving, the phases of Focus, Analyze, Develop and Execute. All participate in the use of the tools of CQI. It is a process that may be termed structured spontaneity.

Quality action teams mark a culture change of basic nature. They do not act like our current committees, which are organized on a hierarchic basis, with the work ethic and practice of Roberts' Rules. While order is maintained, it is more that of workshops, where the product and productive team are centerpiece. The brainstorming tool of CQI resembles the free association of psychoanalysis, and its force field analysis is a major step in that direction. Unlike psychoanalysis, CQI employs discipline each step of the way, in a mutually determined fashion.

Also in CQI, managers initially have difficulty with the simultaneous leveling of hierarchy and the institution of shared responsibility. However, when top management demonstrates its commitment, a spirited rider generally arises out of a "battlefield democracy," in which the colonel, lieutenant, sergeant, and grunt put their heads and hearts together, in common cause.

Given the best of intentions, we can expect the quality action teams, which are being formed to solve specific organizational problems, such as redundancy, or record-keeping, or the handling of charts, to go about their tasks exceedingly slowly, impeded by unfamiliarity with CQI techniques and adherence to the committee ways of the past. This will be especially so, as managers and therapists work on the supremely complex problems encountered in the treatment of the severely disordered.

When all personnel joined in task oriented working groups to change the system, or way of working, the prime "productive circle" is elevated and brought center stage. At ASH, this prime circle is the treatment team. Of course, there are many other productive circles, such as those of the program managers, the unit supervisors, the discipline staffs, etc. However, they all may be conceived to be in support of the treatment team, which is primarily responsible for management of the patient and his groups. I predict that our treatment teams will need the least CQI training of any other working groups at ASH. While to most the nature of CQI is a source of great puzzlement, successful treatment teams have been working in the CQI manner. They are no strangers to brainstorming, freely putting the pieces of the puzzle together, testing *ad hoc* solutions, and changing course in a collaborative way.

The leaders of the treatment teams, the psychiatrists at ASH, have mostly mastered contemporary medication. As leaders, yet in common with the other disciplines, psychiatrists are challenged to master the current advances of the psychosocial rehabilitation approach and its therapeutic community underpinning. Medication eases the therapeutic task immeasurably, through stabilization of our patients in mood, thought and behavior, rendering them more capable of dealing with the stress of living in reality.

But therapy is done basically through the human transaction of personnel and patients, in which the patient is reconciled to reality and the human condition, then habilitated through education and skills trainings in dealing with that reality. For some patients, all that is needed is medication; released from the biological portion of their illness they come back to themselves and reality on their own. For most, alienated for some time, and experiencing the failures of several previous tiers of treatment, the therapeutic task is more daunting, involving buyout psychosocial rehabilitation, a complex of medication, development of therapeutic ties, re-socialization, and re-education.

Many psychotic and most psychopathic individuals will comply with the predominant system, "make do" with that order, waiting for it to weaken and pass. In time, they mold it to their alienated ends, resulting in small societies built on suppression, repression, and degradation of the individual—the snake pits and schools for crime we decry. The most obvious example is present in society's massive prisons where, on the one hand, trustees identifying with personnel rule over their fellows, and on the other, prisoners have their own alienated society.

A comparable but not as obvious state of affairs exists in the traditional "asylum," fixating the patient in the system. Cliques similar to those in prison, which "put patients in their place" exist in the personnel, despite their best efforts at professionalism. It is dawning on us that patients who seem so alienated from one another and the Ward group, are at the same time profoundly influenced by and dependent on that environment. The treatment team is the main force informing the therapeutic relationship with the patient and his group, to guide and enhance their autonomy, essential to further steps in treatment.

As leader of the treatment team, psychiatry has the task of not only diagnosing morbidity per DSM-III, but also of how it manifests itself in the person of the patient. This involves the individual self-concept, relationships with others, life careers and roles, skills and capacities, his very soul. Most of our treatment teams already attempt to operate in such fashion, but are handicapped by excessive patient load and insufficient resources.

The psychosocial rehabilitation approach calls for even more systematic assessment based on those considerations. Again, it calls on us to consider the patient as a person in need of skills to handle specific roles, and empowered to take charge of his life, to his capacity. Their success in such a venture will depend on our capacity to, as relatively autonomous professionals, work out a partnership with the patient population based on attainment of therapeutic community and our capacity to individuate our efforts. Otherwise, we may see the psycho-education of PSR turn into rote schooling and vain social engineering, in which "outcome driven" becomes just that, processing people through the system as occurs too often in modern education.

Ideally, the "normalization" of PSR calls for an acknowledged working relationship with the patients in his rehabilitation group. One may ask, "How can one conduct a normal conversation with a regressed schizophrenic or a hardened psychopath?" An answer lies in the experience of therapeutic community, and also in the one-to-one demonstrations of clinicians like Sullivan, Fromme-Reichmann, Rosen, and Searles. Rosen, speaking directly, in what he called direct psychoanalysis, could evoke sparkling conversation with a deeply stone-like catatonic individual. All of those pioneers were able to transact at the same time in both our and the patients' reality. October, 1992.

Change of System and Individual

CQI holds it is the system that needs fixing, and cautions against undue attention to individual personnel. While this approach keeps us from criticism and perhaps scapegoating of rigid individuals, it deflects attention from their plight. A level, convivial playing field is of great threat to an authoritarian who was not used to contemporary give-and-take. On the other hand, personnel who are used to doing only as they are told may be in terror of speaking up, for fear of transgression, also of bossing others around.

Changes in characteristic ways, which may call for changes in character itself, are stressful. We can expect individual and group crises, which are best dealt with through anticipation. The stresses occasioned by systemic changes call for formation of a support network, stemming from all sectors and levels of personnel, but mostly management. Management, in whom ultimate power and decision lies, needs to understand the underlying realities and the approaches which may have already been developed in crisis intervention and posttraumatic stress management.

The debriefing of crisis intervention calls for more than going over the traumatic situation and reacting. It involves aid to the stressed personnel in dealing not only with current crises, but in mourning losses incurred earlier in their careers, when initial idealism gave way to professionalism. When we mobilize the ideals of personnel, through CQI and TIP, we incur risks and responsibilities. The foregoing processes are comparable with those developed in reaching out and "debriefing" those living in the separate reality of the mentally ill, differing mostly in degree. ASH, in common with American industry and the mental health profession, is developing a new reality, and is setting a pace for the mental health treatment of the next millennium. The break with the past, and also present, is bound to be difficult. ~ 1992.

Changes in Our Way of Doing Therapy

Quality improvement hopefully will bring about the kind of culture change that will position ASH for basic improvement of its treatment. Treatment is what ASH is really about. Admittedly, we serve the people of California by safely containing the most seriously disordered of its antisocial mentally ill, but our prime function is to change them for the better, to reverse their states of alienation, and enable them to adapt successfully to their futures.

We have been doing so since 1954, with advances and retreats. Psychiatrists were at the helm at first, and the patients were mostly sex offenders. We now treat the broad range of psychopathology appropriate to a maximum security hospital. On the other hand, we consider that the structured setting of prison is the one most appropriate for the treatment of the hardened psychopath.

How have we gone about our treatment? From the first, we have provided a secure setting, significantly different from prison. We have let the new patient know that he is in a hospital, and will treat him as well as he will let us. Most, having broken with reality, suffer from alienation from self and others, making it difficult to care for them. For some, we have to stop short of complete physical and psychiatric examination, until they come around to care enough to cooperate with the physician. Along the way, our treatment teams have strived to structure individual and group life away from prison and street culture, through organized therapeutic community and individually prescribed groups, with varying success. The members of the multidisciplinary teams have assessed and ideally formed relationships with the individual patient. Their joint efforts have generally exerted a powerfully therapeutic effect on the person, as well as provided an in-depth and composite view. It is through this group and individual relationship that the person is reconciled to reality and self. Medication is vastly helpful in stabilizing the person in such reality.

Why change this system? Answer: it may not be broken, but it needs fixing, mostly through further development. We have learned from our trial competency units that outcome orientation, a central organizing principle of the new TIP, is extremely helpful in mobilizing patients to focus on personal and group reality. Though acutely ill, they can be reached and taught fairly complicated material, and to face the reality of their situation enough to return to court. A case can therefore be made for reaching the higher functioning patients on the other custody-oriented and prison-based units, by means of psychosocial rehabilitative methods, mobilized and motivated by therapeutic community.

While we are always assessing and reassessing our patients, we need to work out systematic ways to state how they master the tasks of their lives, what we are preparing them for. Psychosocial rehabilitation has made advances in that regard, as well as in procedures, called training modules, to accomplish those tasks. We need to work out the systematics of motivating our patients for their outcomes to develop the autonomous selves essential to that motivation. We need to develop ways of tracking how our patients deal with their future lives, calling for a working relationship with personnel in a multitude of agencies.

ASH will have to turn into a continuous training workshop to enable its personnel to develop themselves and their programs enough to meet those challenges. The personnel themselves will have to do their training and learn how to do the research necessary for basic improvement. ~ 1992.

The Culture Clash at ASH

During its first phase of development, ASH treated mostly sex offenders. Without the outcome studies inherent to TIP, it considered itself successful, until one of its graduates offended grossly. The resulting scandal turned ASH away from treatment of sexual offenders to a general forensic population. In a largely unrelated development, and in common with its sister California State Hospitals, it passed from medical hierarchy and control to the current matrix organization. Now, the psychiatrist is in charge of the patients' treatment, and administration is in charge of the rest.

Theoretically the administration was there to back up and serve the psychiatrist and treatment team in their therapeutic function. However, regression of the Reagan era from the earlier therapeutic community way led to an undue need for control of violent patients by groups of psychiatric technicians. An inverse hierarchy resulted from dependence of the other professions on them.

While recognizing the need for safety of all as the underpinning of treatment, the treatment teams have, in contradistinction, aimed towards control through the therapeutic relationship. Therein lies the "culture clash" that CQI gives promise of mitigating, perhaps ending; for it aims at joining administration and treatment in close partnership through its quality circles, which resemble those in therapeutic community. The treatment aspect of our special treatment plans is taking center stage, by administrative *fait* from outside the hospital, just as we are developing towards that end. ~ 1992.

Developments in Diagnosis and Treatment

Neuroscience research is turning up organic defects in psychotic populations, most likely stemming from early trauma. In the resultant syndrome, the individual would have, for adaptive purposes, transcended such a defect through biologic and psychologic means, generally manifested as personality disorder. Personality disorder renders the individual liable to decompensation and psychosis when developmental stress occurs. Recovery from that psychosis would result in return to the premorbid personality. We see that phenomenon in alcoholism and psychopathy, when, on recovery from their acute episodes, they revert to their prior personalities. Treatment then calls for deeper characterological change, to afford the individual a "safer" hold on reality.

Organizations such as Al-Anon and Children of Alcoholics, also many drug programs, seek such basic personality change, through their therapeutic community-based group life. They provide extraordinary motivation and a structured, family-based regimen to effect changes in the drug dependent personality. At bottom is an effort to free the individual from the alienated identity at the core of the personality disorder, with the eventual freedom from the need for the treatment.

Whether our psychotic population, with its increasingly evident biologic defect, can aspire to such emancipation is problematic. We can attest to the need as with the alcoholics and drug addicts for extraordinary motivation and a structured regimen to help the psychotic personality let go of an identity that has, from this point of view, kept it from psychosis. The recovery movements and the waves of mental hospital reorientation of the hospital personnel toward collaborative action was led by charismatic individuals within and outside of the healing professions, pointing to the role of charisma in the transcendence of the severely disordered state. A similar case can be made for the fewer and short-lived successes in prison treatment.

The modern recovery movements are now more than half a century old. For two centuries prior, society had witnessed waves of mental hospital reform. These developments were led by inspired leaders from within and outside the healing professions. The practitioners of moral treatment in the early 19th century and this century's Alcoholics Anonymous movement held that identification with a deistic principle or object was necessary to treatment, as a stabilizer and motivator of the altered and depleted personality. However, there is definite and successful movement beyond that orthodoxy.

What those movements have in common is what I considered to be the essential motivator: principled, altruistic profession and dedication to one's fellow man. This motivation is what is at the core of the profession of medicine, indeed of the professions in general ("I swear by Apollo. . .".). In its extreme manifestation, it is frankly messianic in nature. It is not by chance that most mental hospital wards have a full-blown or partially identified Christ, and his opposite, the Devil, incarnations of that which they seek.

My thesis is that when American psychiatry became "scientific," just before the Civil War, it shut itself off from an essential element of the therapeutic relationship with significant elements of its patient population. Thus abandoned, that population fell back on itself, into regression, and the asylum became a warehouse. Under the regimen of moral treatment, patients had transcended their psychoses through belief in their doctors and laypersons, who were most likely unconsciously messianic. My corollary thesis is that the psychiatrists and the allied professionals can be messianic and scientific at the same time, provided they maintain appropriate professional safeguards.

Another corollary thesis is that the motivation of many professionals is in part messianic at the inception of their careers. When this is later denied and disavowed, much at the behest of faculty, then peers, that motivational dynamic goes underground, and appears later in disillusionment, burn-out, and perversity. Preventive medicine here would call for a form of professional identity analysis at the inception of one's professional career, to facilitate later natural maturation of what in psychoanalysis is called the ego ideal.

It is not by chance that training for the facilitator role in CQI involved, at the start, exchanges on our underlying motivation in our work, done in a light, jocular, but significant manner. The 20 personnel chosen to become facilitators, through their idealism quickly engaged in the therapeutic community mode, and have felt close since. ~ April, 1993.

The Treatment Alliance

The treatment alliance is of central importance in the treatment of the emotionally disordered. The concept sprang from the recognition, of the development of Freudian ego psychology, that one needed to pay attention, theoretically and in application, to the patient as an autonomous person. This person collaborated with the analyst on his problems, rather than serving as a subject for psychological dissection. The analyst and analyzed negotiated into a relationship in which the factors and vectors leading to alliance outweighed those that were disruptive.

That alliance positioned them, interpersonally and intra-psychically, to accomplish the changes necessary to alleviation and cure of disorder, and adaptation to personal and social reality. Inherent in the process were resistances to change occasioned by the character of the individual, inner conflicts, and that stemming from the past which obviated adaptation to present reality, or transferences. Working out the resistances in the relationship, especially those which tie the individual to the past, again, of transferences, results in increased function in present reality.

Psychotic and psychopathic individuals suffer from severely altered egos, which interfere with adaptation to current reality. Examples are fragmentation and schism within the personality (the schizophrenic process), and compensatory role assumptions of mythic nature (religious and political). It might be stated that reality is too much for them, and they hold themselves to be special people, above, below, and apart from the rest of us. That is why the repositioning of the treatment alliance is so pertinent. Being part of the human group again would entail experiences which they had to transcend to maintain any ego integrity. It is from such a dilemma that we often find the psychotic state worsened when insight therapy is attempted without the treatment alliance that safeguards the ego of the patient.

This treatment alliance relies on the extraordinary motivation utilized in the earliest therapeutic communities, in which that aspect of the personalities of the professional joins to form a sense and state of community. In some cases, this sense of community is frankly messianic; the professional allows self, *pro tem*, to be Savior. The professional is ultimately responsible in this compact, but calls for shared responsibility, as the patient restitutes.

The Evolution of the Treatment Team

Recognizing reality, psychiatry from the first formed a team with nursing. It was highly authoritarian. Then they recognized the need for occupational therapy and social work. Only later did they recognize the team's separate existence in work with the patient. Reality dictated that, without the alliance of professionals in the modern treatment team, psychiatry would be powerless in the treatment of psychosis. Even then, he would have to keep up with the growing disciplines of social work, nursing, rehabilitation therapy, and psychology.

Another aspect of reality is the fact that the members of the team, and the patient population are developing and negotiating their relationship with one another. This complex of considerations is present in the treatment alliance formed by the treatment team with the patient and his group. Each discipline increasingly contributes to this biopsychosocial diagnosis and the treatment plan derived from it. They join in development of an assessment instrument that makes sense to all.

Ideally, as a relatively autonomous participant in the process of alliance and its code is determinative of its outcome, the patient, to his capacity, joins in this diagnostic assessment and treatment plan process. With many, if not most, alienation from self and others interferes. The superior cognitive and motivational capacities of the therapeutic community group provide the team with another restitutive factor. Important in restitution is the mobilization and participation of the patient's previous environment. The drug dependency movements utilize family, friends, and employers to good effect in orienting the lost soul to reality, and motivating him through the treatment. ~ 1992.

A Treatment Team Workshop

As noted earlier, many of ASH's treatment teams have been practicing versions of the advances proposed by the Treatment Improvement Project. Through their constant brainstorming and directness of analysis of situations, they have been utilizing major components of the Continuous Quality Method. In our grand effort at mobilizing how we go about managing ourselves and improving our treatment, we need to call on this primary source, the treatment team, for its expertise in self-improvement. I propose that after the programs and units have reintegrated, we hold a hospital wide workshop devoted to the treatment teams. There we can enable them to go about the task of reconstituting their morale, reevaluating their mission, assessing the treatment programs, and assimilating the PSR method. The workshop could very well be mounted by the Core Services Program, which could utilize the opportunity to work out its relationship with the treatment teams. Such an exercise is in the spirit and method of both PSR and CQI. It would enhance the state of autonomy of the treatment teams, and mobilize enthusiasm necessary to accomplish the massive changes we are asking of them.

A Group Work Training Program

Recognizing the call for a quantum advance in capacity to lead groups of all kinds—motivational and skill training—Ash is in great need of a coherent, hospital-wide training program in group work. The methods of CQI and PSR can be of great help in assessment of need, mobilization of personnel, formulation of curriculum, and development of faculty. This can lead to better assessment by the programs themselves and ongoing monitoring of their changes. I propose we plan such a program to begin after the treatment team workshop.

Conclusions

1. a. Both CQI and TIP are further developments of management and treatment approaches ASH has pioneered since 1954, and give promise to bring us "back on track." They'll do so with the lessened likelihood of regression, their method of mutual participation, call for strong leadership, and backing by society.

   b. CQI consists of problem-solving groups, called quality circles or quality action teams, in which personnel involved in the problem transact in a structured but group dynamic fashion, analyzing, developing, and executing solutions.

   c. In time, this process levels hierarchy, promotes managerial parsimony and regional autonomy, and enhances community spirit. In other words, we at ASH seek to recapture the spirit of enterprise of ASH's early days, when conceivably, management and clinicians were close, if not identical, and tackled problems jointly and directly.

2. a. Our treatment improvement project also is a group venture, in which the treatment team focuses on assessment of the individual patient's adaptive capacity, with a view towards its enhancement through psycho-educational group experiences. It is assessment and outcome oriented.

   b. Both CQI and TIP call for enabling action on the part of ASH as its prime productive circle and furtherance of its development as a group of professionals.

   c. With our chronically psychotic and forensic patients, the question of motivation is essential to improvement. We need to inquire into the nature of the treatment alliance we form with our patients. We need to conduct scientific studies of charisma or messianism in that formation.

3. a. Change *per se* is stressful. Stress is best dealt with through mutual group support and participation, practiced in the context of therapeutic community.

   b. Active participation by management in the facilitation of change is essential.

   c. Failure to do so can result in regression and increased danger in this forensic facility.

4. a. A hospital-wide treatment team workshop is proposed, to mark recognition by ASH of the centrality of the treatment team as the primary productive unit, and enhance its development and functioning.

   b. A grassroots-based group work training program is proposed, as necessary to the progress facilitated by CQI and TIP. 22 November, 1992.

A Hospital-Wide Group Work Training Program

The improvement in treatment expected of ASH's newly reorganized programs will call for expanded, but also intensified work with groups, for the training and retraining essential to that effort. Given the current budgetary difficulties, the logical avenue would seem to be a group work training program taught by the considerable body of personnel now performing group treatment. Accordingly, I would like to propose a hospital-wide multidisciplinary group work training program to be initiated under the auspices of the Core Program Services, which would offer administrative support. If such would not be feasible, it would be based on the Training Service. Organization of the venture would be in five phases:

1. Formation of a multidisciplinary steering group, consisting of the disciplines' chairs, or their appointees, plus an administrative member.
2. After meeting sufficiently to become a working group, it would conduct a survey of experienced group therapists.
3. From the results of the survey, the steering group would assemble a preliminary faculty. This group would meet long enough to become a working entity. The criteria of such would be attainment of a state of mutual confidence and consensus on treatment goals and methods.
4. A group work curriculum would be set forth, including that for psychosocial rehabilitation. A library of textual, audio, and visual material would be established.
5. The faculty would matriculate a multidisciplinary student body, and the first class will begin on a semester basis. Each class would last a year. Each student would be afforded the experience of membership in a training group, conducted along therapeutic community lines.

S/he would be expected to conduct a group, consisting of appropriate patients under individual supervision. A mutual supervisory group would also be part of the curriculum. There would be didactic work throughout the academic year. Attainment of certification would be recognized administratively. December 9, 1992.

A Hospital-Wide Treatment Team Workshop

As its direct link to the patient, ASH's treatment teams are the ultimate focus of concern of both its quality and treatment improvement efforts. They are our basic quality circles. Under development for some time, they are poised for even greater effectiveness, through application of the quality and psychosocial rehabilitative approaches. To that end, the department of psychiatry proposes a workshop which will bring the treatment teams center stage to prepare them for their enhanced rehabilitative role. ASH's "other teams"—administrative, medical, core services, security, dietary and pharmacy—would be represented, to symbolically and functionally supply evidence for their supportive role. In effect, the workshop would, in accordance with CQI, serve to level and realign the working entities at ASH to accomplish their tasks directly and creatively. To convene and organize the workshop, a steering committee is needed. The "team" of the discipline chiefs, or their appointees, would seem appropriate, plus an administrative facilitator. Their tasks would be:

1. Agreement as to the tasks of the workshop
2. Establishment of the mandate and nature of the plenary or workgroup, and its probable task forces or subgroups
3. Convening of the group
4. Acceptance and publication of the workshop report

The tasks of the plenary group may be stated to be:

1. Assessment of the state of the treatment teams at ASH
2. Assessment of the therapy performed on the units
3. Demonstration and assimilation of the PSR method
4. Compilation and analysis of data, and preparation of a workshop report

Because of the large number of treatment teams, it would seem necessary to have no more than two representatives from each team, elected by the team. That number comprises 52; adding representatives from medicine, administration, core services, security, dietary and pharmacy, plus the steering committee members would bring the number to 60+. Properly organized, this would seem an appropriate number, large enough to mark the seriousness of purpose, and evoke the leadership potential of its members.

The plenary group would have much to do, and will have to meet at least twice, the first to learn and agree on how to go about tasks of assessment, and the second to put together and draw inferences from the data gathered on the units. In between meetings, the treatment team representatives would orient their teams to look at how they functioned as teams, and comprehensively survey the therapy on their units.

The plenary group would have its internal organization to accomplish its tasks pertinently and directly. It would elect a moderator, consider its task and mandate, and form such subgroups or task forces as to effect its mission. All this can be done readily, from previous experience with workshops, still preserving the autonomy necessary to such an endeavor.

ASH could expect considerable mobilization of interest, even enthusiasm, as the chief product of this exercise. It will certainly help with the leveling or realignment called for in the CQI approach. The assessment procedures and data generated could be expected to aid in development of PSR assessment, but even more, act as a mirror to the units and baseline to the program of the progress anticipated.

Summary

1. This major endeavor is addressed to ASH's need, after the reconstitution of the programs and units into action outcome oriented entities, for reassessment of our main treatment resource: our treatment teams, their therapeutic interventions, and their relationship to ASH's supportive agencies—administrative, CORE, medical, dietary, pharmacy, and protective.

2. In accordance with the CQI and TIP approaches, to deal with this problem, a quality action team, consisting of the participants to a problem is called for. This workshop is in effect such a team. It will consist of representative elements of ASH's 26 treatment teams. Through our closely organized plenary group, they will receive training in assessment of the operational status and therapeutic effectiveness of their teams. They will participate in demonstration and assimilation of the PSR method.

3. Next, the members will return to their units, and together with their teams, they will gather the desired data on the operation of the teams and the units' treatment activities.

4. In the final phase, the members will return to the workshop, calibrate and analyze their data, and prepare the workshop report.

   We can expect that this process will mobilize a great deal of interest, and strengthen the image and identity of the treatment teams. It will inevitably emphasize the centrality of the teams as

ASH's chief therapeutic modality, and coordination with its supportive agencies. The workshop report will provide pertinent data and conclusions. Thus positioned and strengthened in their roles and capacities, our treatment teams can move forward on ASH's considerable treatment agenda. December 6, 1992.

Solving Problems: A Message for Patients

We at ASH are working to help you help yourself. When you don't help yourself, we all lose. We succeed when you are back on your feet, making it in the world. The work of helping you to help yourself is called treatment. Each person's treatment differs because we are all different. You will say, "If we are all different, why do we have to do the same things, like therapeutic community, and one-to-one sessions? Why can't we choose not to?"

The answer lies in the fact that everybody is confined in the same big boat. We do have choice in where that boat goes—forward, backward, in circles, or standing still. We do choose every day how we move that boat, in our voyage of preparation for our lives outside. We also choose how we move inside that boat, as we choose how we move in our lives, and in our relations with people who are important to us.

The question of choice is central. When a person has no choice, he is in a prison, mental or physical. The issue is how one exercises that choice, whether one is responsible to self and others.

In treatment, we try to get you more involved in the specifics of getting on your feet as persons, to be able to handle your lives, and its many choices. Many of you may be well on your way in that regard. You may have had troubles of one kind or another, in which you made inappropriate choices, but are ok now. You may be positive about going forward with your lives. You may be seeking out opportunities to advance yourself, keeping up with the world through TV, the newspaper, therapeutic community, various groups, and the ASH Community Council.

On your own, you may be preparing to return to court, prison, or community, by figuring out what will be going on there, and how you would handle those situations. Above all, you may have a handle on yourself, and what part you play in your problems.

In working on yourself and problems, you have something in common with the thousands of people who have been patients at ASH since it opened its doors in 1954, to pioneer in the recovery from emotional illness in a forensic setting. ASH has attempted to help them face social reality, but more important, the reality they make for themselves, their individual reality.

But many of you are still in retreat from individual and social reality in one way or another and need special care, including medication, to help restore your capacity and balance. Human beings have, since time immemorial, turned from themselves and their reality in ways accounted as mad. When they turned on other people, they would be judged offensive, even evil. For a long time, the retreat from and turning on reality was blamed on demonic possession by spirits, a matter for religious redemption and efforts to induce or drive those spirits from the sufferer or offender.

We now hold that peoples' difficulty with those realities comes from a combination of learned behavior, innate traits, and biological factors. We are also learning what goes on in people that makes them turn from and against themselves and others. From tentative beginnings, marked by ever-ready backward swings, we are developing ways of dealing with troubled and troubling people, to bring them into their lives. The principle is the same as that of democratic life, the involvement of people in their own destinies.

That involvement calls for a special set of relationships, and a special course of action. In treatment, the patient is relieved of decision-making until he attains the capacity to make his decisions in no way responsible to self and others. This comes as a relief to many patients and prisoners. We run the danger of losing you to some socially ordained limbo of institutionalization if we do not at the same time establish a way of working to help you back to your life and society, to reality. This way of working is called the treatment alliance.

The Treatment Alliance

You will ask, "How can we expect a person who has lost his mind and trust for people to form such a close working relationship?" To form that alliance you need to have a grasp of your situation and to care about helping yourself.

In answer, even in our most regressed and alienated state, we keep in touch with pieces of reality. From them, we can reconstruct new, hopefully better versions. We look for something, someone to save our situation. That saving principle is the basis of the Alcoholics Anonymous movement and that of ex-prisoner groups. There, people draw on strengths to help one another out of their self-destructive situations. Before AA, it was common in the US and still is in many parts of the world for men to ally themselves in drinking groups, reinforcing their self-destructive behavior, and furthering their careers in alcoholism. Prisons, ghettos, and certain segments of society are still dominated by openly anti-social group life.

As in AA and the offender groups, in treatment you are expected to figure out your strengths and weaknesses. Recognition of handicaps is a humbling experience, but even more important is the fact that you work together in the process. You can be powerful in motivating, understanding, and working out change in yourself and your fellows.

Many of your fellow patients are experiencing pieces of what they went through in their time of difficulty. Some are frozen in panicked, death-like states, cut off from the rest of us. Many are caught up in high states of exaltation, then dip into depression. Many are caught up in nightmarish plots and threats that make no sense to the rest of us, but that they hold to be quite real.

We assume that all can respond to firm care and attempts by all patients and personnel to enlist their working together on solution of their problems. We assume that your problems are common to all human beings, to a different degree. Those who have embarked on careers in crime present special difficulty, especially when you have formed strong ties there.

In therapeutic community, the care for one another is similar to that found in religious formations, town hall meetings, and the "the circling of the wagons" of pioneer times. Once you have achieved such alliance, you can, feeling mutual and strengthened, together with personnel, proceed to active healing and put together the pieces of your lives.

The role of personnel is to help you to help yourself. As you help other patients, you help yourself work through aspects of your problems that are only natural for you to want to avoid. But beyond that lies the task of grasping what about yourself led to this turn in your life, and what needs changing. It is likely that such change will call for a long effort with a professional, but the time to start is now. The hospital personnel stand ready to launch you on that journey.

But our prime task is getting you on your feet, and moving on to your next step in your life, be it court, prison, or the community. To that end you can expect a great deal of psychosocial instruction, group and individual, to help you become either competent to stand trial, make it in prison profitably—staying safe, getting educated, keeping up with your family, etc.—or to start your civilian life over again.

So treatment is not anything mysterious. It is a new world of working on human problems that formerly defeated our best efforts. It is you choosing to make sense of your life and situation with the help of others, and choosing to help others to make sense. We understand a great deal now of what formerly was a land of mystery, why people turn on themselves and one another. We are learning more with each passing year, and much of what we learn comes from you. Former patients and offenders are making great contributions, individually and through national and local organizations. Therapy is a joint effort and a matter of choice. 7 February, 1993.

CHAPTER IV

Family Therapy at ASH

A History of Family Therapy and Therapeutic Community

Therapeutic community becomes like a family when it is in full swing. The members display warmth, verbal and physical, likely seen nowhere else but in church gatherings, and those do so through family-like feelings. The family of the patient was welcome to partake in all aspects of therapeutic community.

It is in recognition of this nuclear time between two social systems, family and therapeutic community, that the family members were welcome at treatment team meetings at the state hospitals in California. Family Day at Atascadero State Hospital transforms a ward dayroom into a lively family living room. Not only does the conjunction of family and therapeutic community result in a virtual deinstitutionalization, but it affords the patients this single most potent psychological intervention to their illness.

The natural group process in the therapeutic community group and its therapeutic subgroups result in family-like transactions. There, members have experiences recapitulating traumatic situations of the past, but in a protected setting. Participation of the family itself, as well as friends, teachers, and employers, when it is possible to engage their collaboration, helps the group to attain not only a more secure platform of reality from which to work through deviations, but also more specific focus on the problem at hand.

The problem centers on the capacity of the therapeutic leadership to assemble a group of families, orient it to the task, and manage it through its exacting work. Al-Anon and children of alcoholics had been able to successfully operate as multi-family groups for decades, mostly independent of professional authority and guidance.

An early personal experience with this phenomenon occurred in my work with schizophrenics in a private institution during the 1960s. The group of families in the Hanbleceya therapeutic community considered themselves a community in itself. Like other such social groups, it developed a club-like atmosphere and a certain amount of double-timing within the larger community. As a result, I came to call it the family community group, rather than the usual designation of multi-family group. I thereby emphasized this sense of community that had arisen, and that was its chief underlying dynamic. In my practice and in the literature, it consisted of a number of families, three to as many as a dozen, which met, generally in the context of a therapeutic or correctional community for assistance, with the crises which accompany the onus of a family member.

The crises in the families of this group were generally developmental and family-wide, and marked by autism and alienation, often appearing from under a façade of normalcy. The child was often exemplary until adolescence or early adulthood, the dementia praecox of several generations ago. The mother was a model mother until the onset of delusional melancholia and her daughter's menarche. The father may have been a pillar of the community until a midlife crisis and depressive outcome. All the family was deeply troubled from the start, but transcended its difficulties until growth of its members threaten its often autistic bases of existence.

The development and dissemination of crisis theory, and family therapy, has aided the therapeutic discipline and also our citizenry in their work of amelioration of the human condition. The people in Parents Without Partners have achieved a collective wisdom on the crisis that newly divorcing families can expect to traverse, as have most of the mutual help groups.

Psychoanalysis has contributed immeasurably to crisis theory through its concepts of individual and intergenerational lines of development, and the various modes of ego distortion and functioning. It starts at the beginning, with the pre-Oedipal experience, where the child learns its roles by collaborating and competing, first with his mother in the active nurturance. It next experiences individuation. Then, through the successive outcome of the Oedipal experience, it enters apprenticeship for the role to be played in his/her family to be. After the Oedipal struggle, it finds its place in the world of children and play and practice. It leaves childhood and approaches adulthood as an adolescent, and prepares for a family of its own as an adult. In midlife the individual comes to terms with ties to forebears and terms with the outcome of investment in family and career.

Without a concept of the internal psychic and cognitive workings of the individual, this schema of phases and stages of development would be two-dimensional. In fact, one of the pioneers of systems therapy thinks of the individual as a point in his schema. For all the ambiguities and contradictions of its theories, psychoanalysis has given depth to developmental theory, an approach to the individual in the system. Chief among its contributions are its structural theory, in which it considers the relation of the conscious to the unconscious, a hypothesis of an operant ego, and the latter-day contributions of the interpersonal and intra-psychic object relations. These new conceptions led to an understanding of how one takes in one's family environment, how one maintains the self, and the subsequent developmental crises.

Freud posited an archaic family, the Primal Horde, which comes close in size to the upper limits of our family community, and has some of the characteristics of the clan. In his construct, the father was the originator and head of a number of subfamilies, ruling and sexually servicing them all. Excluded from their proper roles, his sons murdered, then ate him, and placed him as a totem God.

This fantastic story has commanded the serious attention of anthropologists and religionists for its explanatory value. There seems to be something to the thesis of oral incorporation reflected in the village's ritual, human sacrifice, and the evolution of the Godhead. More than that, in their crises and regression in moral rites and functioning, the families of the mentally ill take on the characteristics of this primal family, the primal horde, incestuous object ties, sole reigning head who was martyred, and an autistic ego ideal, with a primitive God.

A follower of Freud, J.C. Flugel, studied the family from a theoretic point of view in the psychoanalytic study of the family (1921)—what came to be known a quarter of a century later as systems theory in his description of the Oedipal family system and the herd collectivity. To this he added to Freud's mythology a rather extensive primitive cosmogony that went back to the beginnings of the Greek God system. Most important was his reach into the role of myth in family development, and phenomenon attendance of the intergenerational dynamics, interactions with his mother, plus a three-generational hypothesis.

The love triangle of mother, father, and child figures large in the psychoanalytic treatment diet. An aspect of that, the primal scene, makes its appearance in the psychoanalytic situation, as an aspect of the transference or unfinished business from the past which interferes with current reality. The transference itself, central to psychoanalysis, happens through situations mostly stemming from the experience in the developmental crucible, the family of origin.

Despite these family-relevant considerations, the family itself has been excluded from the psychoanalytic encounter. Such would be an intrusion in the free associative and regressive processes impugning the purity of clarity of the emerging material. Psychotic, psychopathic, and borderline individuals were judged unsuitable for psychoanalysis.

In the great emergency that was World War II, a number of analysts and analysts-to-be worked with these excluded individuals, freely utilizing modifications of the psychoanalytic method, one of which was group therapy. I was fortunate to have been inducted into the therapeutic community approach, modified for a correctional community. Following my band, I developed a multi-therapist approach which was to presage the work reported in this chapter. The results of our correctional community were extremely encouraging; ardent and alienated prisoners were reconciled to Army service.

After the war, the approach developed in that crucible was of service in work with maximum security and other patients at St. Elizabeth's Hospital. We developed a hospital-wide multi-disciplinary training program in group therapy. On one of the wards for the chronically ill, a spontaneously formed group of female patients and their mothers sat me down to discuss their problems. I noticed a remarkable increase in the patient capacity to verbalize, and a corresponding one in the morale of the mothers. Out of it came a two-year therapeutic encounter and a research report, Maternal Dependency and Schizophrenia.

This led to several full-scale multi-family groups at St. Elizabeth's, at several clinics, and at the National Institute of Mental Health (NIMH). The results were promising and became a long-term feature of most of those programs. The most elaborate one took place at NIMH, where the chief of service, a half dozen therapists, and 40 family members and patients met in a highly interactive and personalized encounter.

Those ventures uniformly reported a heightened sense of purposefulness and morale of the family members and patients, and reorientation to their situations. Reaching a jointly arrived-at understanding of their family's situation, they experienced a mandate to transact on issues in each other's lives. They reflected their observations and interpretations in the group process and formed alliances in helping one another.

Based on successes achieved in the group, they sought further counseling and psycho-therapy as families and individuals. This effect was to render the manifest patient more accessible to depth psychological intervention. Multidisciplinary in nature, the groups were also useful in training therapists, and in bringing the disciplines together in action.

I have used the family community approach in my private practice, in a derivative group formation, couples groups, and work with extended, at times as many as four, generational families.

It is interesting that couples groups per se become the principal approach of Murray Bowen, one of the pioneers in family and multi-family therapy and the most prominent contributor to its literature. Bowen started a five-year project in 1955 at the NIMH, consisting of entire families that lived under observation in a clinical setting.

Individual families lived there for as long as 40 months. He was attempting to search out the family's role in the genesis and alteration of the schizophrenic state. Under the first year of the experiment, the mothers and patients were given analytically-oriented individual therapy. Next, the family was studied as the unit of illness, and fathers were required to join the living unit.

The research endeavor lasted several months, becoming a community per se—families, research and treatment staffs. Communication became open, and all records and meetings were open to all. The therapists and families were enthusiastic, but impasses occurred. In the last year, Bowen called on one family to speak at a time, silencing any others, so that they could "listen."

Bowen continued to use the multi-family group to which patients were referred by the local school system and juvenile court, with mediocre results. Bowen complained that too much time was spent on parents' complaints about the child, and terminated the venture in a year, without any deep-seated changes that he saw.

Upon this rich history of therapeutic family support groups, the program at ASH was built.

Background

In his vision for ASH, Dr. Rood failed to include the patient's family in his grand design. It is understandable, given how it complicates security. He certainly brought about a family spirit, as evidenced by his regular epistles. They came from a benign father figure, especially in regard to the psychiatrists he sought to attract to this out-of-the-way retreat.

His inspirational presence and communications bore fruit, resulting in patient government, a farm program, and family visits in the large visiting room. But the first organized family program did not occur until the early 1970s. Albert Goodman, PhD and Edward Bird, MSW formulated a family program, to be located on two wards: U 27 and U 28. It was approved administratively, initiated, then moved to U 25 and U 26, for their proximity to the trailers. They were requested but not authorized until 1982.

At one time, the family treatment program had its own director, from 1972 until his resignation in 1976 over differences stemming from changes in the treatment of sex offenders. The program continued, and a variety of approaches prevailed, from classroom communication of data, to medication, moral reeducation, healthful living, transactional analysis, psychodrama, and family sculpting.

Psychiatrists were in short supply (one per program), as were psychologists. Social workers, nurses, and psychiatric technicians carried the program. At one time 46 families were involved. Two trailers were assigned for conjugal visits, preceded by two hours of intensive counseling. At one memorable family day there were 120 patients and family members in all, in the U 25 day room, where the lined-up tables filled the space.

A team made up of psychiatrists, social workers, and psychologists collaborated in the mid-1980s in developing the program to its highest and most consistent point. Meeting monthly, there were two multi-family groups, one of which was Hispanic, intensive individual family sessions, and much activity, centering on the family visits in the trailers. A weekly family seminar met the training needs of the professional personnel.

This came to an end in 1992, apparently due to security considerations and also dis-affection on the part of the level-of-care personnel on U 25. Formerly, level-of-care personnel were enthusiastic participants and initiators.

The Family Support Group Project at ASH

The work continued in abbreviated, but still significant form in a large visiting room and new treatment area, Room Number One. Myself and a social worker met with individual families in the large visiting room, and later as a multi-family group. The post-session attendance grew more sparse, as did the number of personnel.

A number of dedicated families continued. Many were members of CAMI (California Alliance on Mental Illness), and they reached out to one another between sessions. Two became members of the hospital advisory board.

A typical session consisted of four to five families. This resulted in a group of 15 to 17 occasionally, and at its largest, 24. It was held in a circle and lasted for one half to two hours. In any one session, the attendees included several long-term families who exhibited the sort of motivation and person-to-person interaction found in the anonymous self-help movement—reaching out to new members, and affording each other emotional support. It was helpful to have the professionals on hand to guide the members.

There were systematics to the group transactions, established by generations of therapists and families. There was a self-introductory phase, one for the accounts of immediate concerns and the transactions to deal with them, and a phase of discussion of shared problems the group wanted to study.

Families uniformly expressed gratification at the end of sessions, saying they had relief from burdens of excessive guilt, isolation, or helplessness. They had acquired information for how to go about dealing with the alienation that beset them, how to deal with crises, as well as knowledge of mental illness and psychopathy, including medication management.

It must be understood that the work done by the personnel, from the beginning, was in addition to assigned duties. It had come become evident to them that collaboration of families in treatment resulted in a quantum advance, and that insight was now recognized. These have been the cutting edge advances made at ASH, against considerable resistance by aspects of administration and also level-of-care personnel and indifference on the part of the professional staff. It must be pointed out that the family project is a prime example of both BPSR and CQI, long prior to their advent at ASH.

The aim of the family support group team was the demonstration of its method in a centrally situated program, on the way to its adoption elsewhere in the hospital. The team presented colloquia and reports to the professional staff, plus calls for an enlistment of families and team members. Systematics were worked out relative to referral of families and administrative monitoring. Personnel were gradually informed as to the existence of the program and referred new families. What follows is a summary of the Family Support Group Project (FSGP), originally written by Elisabeth Abrahams, MFT, at ASH, during the early 1990s:

"Drawing from ASH's patient population through referrals by personnel, the FSGP served to orient families to their supportive function, then assembled them in a multi-family support group, meeting once a month.

Open-ended in nature, membership ranged from two to ten families, and group sessions were conducted along therapeutic community lines, structured psycho-educationally, and focused on the supportive function. Employing the therapeutic processes of ventilation, catharsis, and mutual identification, it served to position its members in their cognitive and emotional reality.

The Project Team consisted of a Director, Coordinator, and several team members (psychiatrist, psychologist, social worker, rehab therapist), using Hospital Protective Services for security backup. In addition to leading, recruiting members, and keeping other hospital personnel informed of its progress, the team was also engaged in furthering the use of family support activities in other programs, hospital-wide.

In its first year, members exhibited symptoms of disjunctive communication, alienation, conflicted relations, and overly dependent ties. Goals included motivation and commitment among members to attend and participate regularly; the exchange of present orientation to their situations and one another; the development of the capacity to support each other and to lessen conflict and alienation; and to demonstrate competence in supportive behavior and the resolution of family concerns.

These goals were measured by attendance records, observed listening and feedback skills, observed empathy and identification with each other's situations; and statements of tenable courses toward resolution of identified difficulties in their relationships.

Methods such as didactic group instruction, plus discussion of suggested related readings and audiovisual materials were used. A total of eight meetings were held the first year, with positive results. Members reported feeling the group was worthwhile, with concerns addressed and often alleviated. Members also reported unanimously that they wanted to meet again the following month."

However, another policy change, secondary to security considerations, resulted in restriction of the group to the large visiting room. The ambient noise generated by several families visiting had not significantly interfered with the individual family sessions, but rendered the multi-family sessions extremely difficult. Attendance decreased.

There was a core constituency of five dedicated families, despite the discharge of the long-term patients. During a temporary hiatus, only two families attended.

Family Support Group Session Summary—Ward 25, 1996.

26 participants were seated in a wide semi-circle including 5 staff and 21 family members. These were the wives, brothers, sisters, and parents of the patients. The session ran about 1 hour and 45 minutes; ASH patients were brought in during the second half. The session opened with self-introductions all around. Staff included Drs. Satu and Abrahams, ward psychiatrists, plus two social workers and a therapist. The following is a synopsis of the various conversations that took place, in the order that they occurred.

Dr. Abrahams asked one father how he felt when his son stormed out of the group during a previous session. Family member speculated he was reacting to his brother's suicide. Others talked about how it felt to discover there was something wrong with their loved one's minds; one expressing anger that he wasn't told before. Now many are optimistic because they at least know why their relatives did what they did. One father was pleased to see his son upbeat and responding well to the schedule and routine at the hospital. He felt his son was participating and that made him feel more upbeat. He was happy his son was taking more responsibility and had moved up a level.

Everyone agreed that all their patient-relatives seemed better today. One reported her son is eating better; has stopped gaining so much weight. He's more concerned with his appearance; looking after himself; caring more about himself . . . which means he is getting well. He's on new medication and "his hands look so clean!" He's paying attention to what's going on.

Dr. Satu reported that three families have experienced positive advances but it hasn't always been that way. They have been through hard times. How does one survive? he asks. How does one enjoy these advances without fear? How do they cope with the changes?

A mother admits she's always afraid something's going to happen. She prays and she's happy things are getting better but she's always on guard. She's afraid to be too happy. A wife agreed with her. She has to take it one day at a time.

One wife says her husband is coming home soon so his therapy has been escalated. She has expectations and says it's difficult to see the difference between demands and expectations.

A mother whose son is at Level 3 says her son is very agitated. She never knows how it's going to be. There's tension that has a domino-effect. This open community has helped her. Because now she discusses her son's illness openly with group members and others.

One family stated it's hard for them come to the hospital and then not be able to see their loved one. A member suggested joining the Alliance for the Mentally Ill in their area. It has helped them. They say it's hard to drive all this way for just a half hour with their son. The doctors tell them it's just part of his illness. That helped them understand better but it's very hard. "I was very ignorant for a long time."

"It's hard for me to accept mental illness," said one woman. "Now I know it's there, but I was in denial a long time." She told the group her son had depression and a suicidal breakdown; that she was terrified. "I don't know if I'm feeling shame or if I'm afraid of it or what." She has always been afraid of people who are mentally ill. Now her son is calling her to ask "What would you do if I committed suicide?" She said she had to let go and let God. That's how she operates.

Another mother identified with her. She was in denial too; then felt guilty. Now she doesn't. "It's not our fault."

Another woman said, "Never think you are alone. The more you talk, the less afraid you are. Time helps too."

One woman added, "Mental illness is such an inside thing. Our son hasn't gone backwards yet. He accepts the label schizophrenic and we don't talk about the voices very much."

There is very even / equal participation from all the group members. It is a well-balanced session. Therapist Elisabeth Abrahams gently asks the woman speaking if she knows what schizophrenia means? Then she explains it's from the Greek, meaning broken or split soul or spirit. She then suggests that we all have souls and that they're all a little broken. Some are so broken they need more help. That's the way she thinks about mental illness.

Dr. Satu asks what prompted the one son to ask his mother what her response to his suicide might be. The mother said he told her he was suicidal; that talking to staff didn't help. She told him it was his choice; that she couldn't be with him 24 hours a day. She did not call the staff. She said she had no fear of life and death.

Dr. Satu asks her if she's had that kind of interchange with her son in the past. She replied "It depends on where he's at and where I'm at."

A woman said, "No one should ever feel ashamed to have a family member with mental illness. If my son had been suicidal, I would have called staff immediately. They see our loved ones every day. It takes the burden off you. They have broad shoulders."

One member mentioned there had been a suicide at the hospital and it had affected everyone. One mother used to blame herself but not anymore. She now calls staff and reports these moods. Dr. Abrahams asks the first mother if she felt she need to save him. She said yes. They'd talked about it in therapy. "He wants me to make him happy but I can't do that for him. He's starting to see the world doesn't revolve around him but it's taken a long time."

A social worker asks a father: "All this suicide talk. How do you feel?"

He replies: "I don't worry anymore like I used to. The church says suicides go to heaven, not hell, if they're not in their right mind."

One mother offers: "It's hard to accept mental illness. It just gets worse and worse. In court, they get laughed at by the judges. That made me so mad, they are so ignorant. They thought they were educated. Our son was barefoot, holding up his pants. They laughed at him; he looked awful. I can't understand how well-educated people can laugh like that. I was having trouble handling mental illness, but to see these officials laughing . . . it was so callous."

A woman adds: "They treat mental illness worse than bank robbers. You can be shuffled off. No one cares; he doesn't matter. People get mad at me for staying with him. I would rather work it out than walk away. You can't just throw them away."

A woman: "I would tell the suicidal person NO you can't do that." Another: "I got angry."

The first woman: "By the time I got off the phone, he was saying he wouldn't do it. I was comfortable with that. He's made numerous attempts." "You're just worn out," a woman said.

Other members offered up their own experiences with attempted suicides. Methods and results were discussed.

"I used to think it was wrong to have those feelings [suicide]," said a man. "He thinks it's wrong too. I'm learning to deal with my feelings now and not think of them as right or wrong. I accept him as he is. That's very important for him right now because we've rejected him in the past. I'm feeling some positive things with him. I'm trying to understand where he's coming from. There's a real parallel between us. I've just come out of treatment for alcoholism. I am so moved and touched by him. The support is there."

Another man: "We get core messages when we're kids. Boys don't cry, don't talk, don't be, don't exist. That's the message I got. It's hard. I know being able to express these feelings has helped me. It's helping him too. I don't know why I didn't die that night" [referring to a suicide attempt].

A woman: "You need to be here!"

A man: "There's a lot of pain in the soul. I see our family coming together like a birth. It's painful. I couldn't imagine my kids going through this. All I know is there's been growth in our family over these 2 years; acceptance of being who you are—there's something about that."

Break—patients join their families in the session. Dr. Satu welcomes them.

Dr. Abrahams recaps the discussion of suicide, hard times, and feelings.

A mother tells her son she shared his suicidal phone call with the group. "I was angry," she said. "It was hard for me to accept this dual diagnosis of alcoholism and mental illness."

Patient: "I had my first overdose at ten years old. I have 25 attempts on my record. I took drugs. I cut myself up. It was a cry for help. I know 15 people who've committed suicide. I talked to one of them for hours. I feel like I am made of the same material as them; that's my destiny. My family loves me. I think about the pain I felt when my friend did it; my family would feel the same way. Suicide is not the way out. It gets better little by little. I'm thankful. It takes guts to be here."

Dr. Abrahams: "Part of what we feel is survivor's anger. This reflects the angry component of self-destruction. My family loves me. There is tension between anger and love. Love wins out."

A patient talks about a brother who committed suicide. "I hurt so much from that. Right Dad? It's still there. Dad is still mad at him. Yeah, he gave up. I almost want to give up sometimes.

A woman: "What stops you?" Patient: "It would hurt my parents."

Dr. Abrahams: "How did the patients feel when suicides happened on the ward?"

Patient: "I'm more interested in ending my own pain than anyone else. Now I think of others; sometimes the only thing that keeps me from doing it is filling my mind with so much noise I block out everything else."

Another patient: "Sometimes I think of it. What if things get better? Thankfully I didn't. Things weren't bad enough."

Woman: "I've never stopped loving you. It's painful to accept your actions. When you went to Dr. Abrahams and prison I knew you would be raped—a perfect candidate—used and abused." She starts to cry, covers her face; patient son reaches out to calm her. She sobs; he strokes her arm.

Dr. Abrahams: "She's in agony for you."

Woman sobbing: "It was too painful to think of you, to know where you were—and there was nothing I could do. So I decided to (she pushes away the air with her arms)—otherwise I'd die. That's how I dealt with it. I never stopped loving you. I couldn't cope with that. Same with your father. He drinks, but I never stopped loving him. And I'll never stop loving you. You're my son."

Patient son: "I love you too."

Dr. Satu: "This is the first time you've allowed yourself to cry" (she nods)

Dr. Abrahams: "You've shared with us the agony about what is going on in your mind about your son; you couldn't stand what he was putting himself through and what life was putting him through."

Woman: "It's agonizing."

Dr. Abrahams: (to another woman) "You understand?"

Woman: "This is the way she has to cope. I understand that very well. I was scared to death to do that, too."

Dr. Abrahams: "We've just shared a deep emotional epiphany. I don't know how we can achieve closure accept by talking more, but we can't do that; we have to stop."

145

Another woman: "I read an article by Katherine Kubler Ross. She says anger lasts about 15 seconds, then it's over. When you grieve and cry, it's much more lasting. I wish that for you. The weeping happened with your son by your side, with your son comforting you. Healing. Isn't that part of what love is?"

Dr. Abrahams: "By your side but separate . . . you are connected but there are no demands."

Patient: "It's a fascinating feeling. I've been doing time for 18 years. This is the first time I get visitors. Every time they come, it's a feeling like I' m part of a family. I don't have problems in prison. I know how to take care of myself. This is the first time I've heard her talk about this. I'm thankful for that."

One or two other members give closing well wishes to everyone. There are several words of comfort and support. Session ends.

The epiphany at the end of this session, in which mother and son enacted their tender tie, of obvious messianic nature, was present in some form in most of the multifamily group sessions. This powerful mechanism appears to me to be built into the family community experience. The reader is referred to the family community at Hanbleceya reported in *Terra Incognita: Psychoanalytic Exploration of the Human Soul*. To my mind the essential element here is that of therapeutic community, as differentiated from the educational experience that replaced the hospital administration the program cited here.

CHAPTER V

The Psychoanalytic Seminar

The psychoanalytic seminar was held during most of my tenure at ASH. It met monthly, membership ranging from six to twelve, examining pertinent psychoanalytic literature, especially that on malignant transformation, by psychoanalyst Otto Kernberg. Emphasis was placed on its meaning to a community of psychiatrists hitherto largely devoted to mastering medication.

This community of psychiatrists numbering 36 (with the exception of its psychoanalytically inclined members, numbering 5) was convinced of the value of the primary role in therapy of medication for concomitantly schizophrenic and psychopathic. Engaging these mature professionals anew in matters psychoanalytic and epistemological was a daunting challenge. Accordingly, I went back to an experience I had in Howard Hall at St. Elizabeth's in collaborating with a professor of adult education, Dr. John Powell, author of *Education for Maturity*.

There he engaged the maximum security patients in a dialogue centering on the readings of tracks like the Declaration of Independence. The members grew quite eloquent in expressing their opinions; it was amazing how they accepted intellectual discipline in favor of collaborating in American way of each person having their say. Dr. Powell had been inducted into this approach by Dr. Alexander Meiklejohn, and founded with him the experimental college at the University of Wisconsin-Madison. Convinced of the value of this primary approach, I decided to utilize it in initiating the staff conference on the role of psychoanalytic treatment at Atascadero State Hospital. Each professional was to have their say on the emergent data in the context of collaborating with the others to reach a consensus on its meaning. The medical director Dr. Gordon Gritter and Dr. David Saunders, the educational director, concurred on the possible value of this re-educational venture. By the end of my tenure at ASH, we had agreed on the value of listening to the data on intrapsychic and interpersonal phenomena, along with the comparable exercise in meaning expressed in the volume *Listening to Prozac*, a prominent medication we employed. (Powell, 1950, pgs. 213–226)

As elsewhere in this volume, we should place the material in historical context. I can trace my inquiry into matters of characterology with the novelist Dr. Smith Fennimore Cooper and his vivid description of frontiersmen and Indians, as in *The Last of the Mohicans*. Tolstoy in equally vivid fashion describes the simultaneous personal and socio-historic situation in the invasion of Russia by Napoleon. Later, I learned to think in academic historic terms under the tutelage of Professor Bernstein. I cut my scientific teeth in the disciplines of biology and physics, learning the scientific method.

Freud taught that human life, interior and external, can be studied scientifically and I started to do so in a multidisciplinary setting during the Second World War at the Fort Knox Rehabilitation Center for

Military Prisoners. We noted and induced theories to a massive change in the orientation to reality of the prisoners under our ministration. I noted a special intuitive connectedness there as well as the phenomenon of messianism. We identified Freud's theory of the transference, alongside Professor Bernstein's theory of social regression, and progression made the phenomena in the group understandable. Freud's theory of the triangle of mother, father, and child made their vicissitude coherent and somewhat predictable.

Study under Harry Stack Sullivan led me to venture further into a theory of self-alienation and malignant transformation, the latter conceived of by Sullivan to occur towards the end of that first decade. Particularly important was Sullivan's theory of the self, described as the self-system. Another mentor, Ernest Hadley, demonstrated the applicability of dream theory to work with schizophrenics. Personal and professional experience with psychic death and its correlate resurrection provided possible insight into Freud's espousal of the universality of a Death Instinct.

Clinical collaboration with ministers confirmed my emergent theory of messianism. My work with analytic groups and with families confirmed Freud's theory of regression. Support of my call for a psychoanalytic seminar at ASH by Doctors Gritter and Saunders was important in the at first reluctant acceptance by the staff of this "class". In the following narrative we shall be avoiding names of the participants because of difficulties in obtaining clearance.

Soon after I was elected Chair of the Department of Psychiatry, I initiated the seminar on psychoanalysis. The theory and practice of medication had been long attended to by a monthly seminar which employed an outside consultant, plus review committee functions. I still aimed to institute a group work-training committee, which had been superseded by the Treatment Improvement Project, then the Continuous Quality Program, mandated by the department of mental hygiene.

The psychoanalytic seminar met in the Staff Conference Room monthly, for an hour and a half. Generally, six to twelve staff members attended, setting agenda as we went along. The most popular topic was a tape of Otto Kernberg on malignant narcissism. I generally kept notes, from which this report is drawn (*Severe Personality Disorders: Psychotherapeutic Strategies*, 1984, and *Borderline Conditions and Pathological Narcissism*, 1975).

Listed Summaries of Sessions

March 7, 1994

The members agreed to pursue the psychoanalytic theory of aggression. They referred to Freud's *Civilization and its Discontents*, and the task of mastering the instincts of aggression and self-destruction. Some held that aggression may be generated in reaction to frustration, developmental and adaptive, pluralistic and integrative.

In considering the Death Instinct, we came across Freud's concept of *Eros* and *Thanatos*. Their creativity was joined to aggression. At that time I advanced my theory of psychic death, stemming for my researches to date. The following psychoanalytic authors were critical of the Death Instinct: Hartman, Kris, and Lowenstein had brought up the issue of neutralized aggression in the integration of the ego. Waelder had emphasized it as a stimulus and a threat to self-preservation, while Fromm emphasized benign aggression versus malignant aggression, the human propensity to destroy and crave, eventuating in relative control. One result was a specific character disorder, necrophilia. Kohut was brought up as a prime contributor in self-psychology in the genesis of aggression. He also offered a developmental hypothesis, regarding an inherent need or empathetic response from the nurturing one to the infant. In addition, Winnicott was noted for his contribution to mutuality. In his concept of the holding environment, he has the early ego tending to split vertically, into good and bad. Finally, the seminar at some length studied Kernberg who elaborated on this subject of narcissism, emphasizing a malignant form.

April 8, 1994

A following seminar dealt with the impossibilities in treatment. A member brought up experience at the beginning of his career with a patient who compulsively cut his wrists. He was addicted to barbiturates following a long career in reformatories. He tore out the stitches that followed the cutting episodes. He presented a problem in management based on an apparent willingness to pay any price to get his way.

A member stated that one is helpless when one's son is persistently defiant. I gave an example of a prisoner who stated that he had no choice but to risk death in defying authority—he "had to." I cautioned explaining away the motivation of the patient on superficial grounds. Members held that psychopaths in extreme form are willing to die for their cause.

In contradiction, a member cited a case of a psychopath who arrived at a pro-social, altruistic solution to his dilemmas. There was evidence there of a therapeutic alliance. I then brought up the case of a colleague who was honored in reconciliation on his deathbed by a prisoner of 25 years before. Several examples of deeply resistive patients emerged in the discussion, one of whom became massively schizophrenic when he lost his psychopathic defenses. Members agreed with this, in their experience, stemming from "powerful life scripts."

Members agreed that one of the patients, Calendar, was underneath it driven to suicide. His extreme resistance to conformity made appearance in court impossible. I then cited the concept of "the therapeutic despair," stemming from such behavior, as indicative of an underlying intention on the part of the patient. Emancipation from fixation in that struggle would be entailed. A transcendent consideration there was keeping the patient alive. Members cited instances of solutions to those dilemmas in their experience. The seminar ended on the note of Freud's Theory of the Death Instinct as underlying the compulsivity of the cases cited by the members. Members agreed that they had experienced enmeshment with that compulsive imperative when they felt helpless, and through that counter-transference, they conceived what the transference was. What might be the transference?

May 7, 1994

At my instance we discussed the book, *Makes Me Want to Holler*—by Nathan McCall, a black male, from a particular ghetto in LA, a dysfunctional family, drugs, and gangs. He took his aberrant way of life for granted. Then he came to a critical point in confrontation with a rival group whose leader insulted him concerning ancestry. His response was to acquire a gun. He shot him in a cultural self-esteem action. McCall felt exhilarated about killing him, but it dawned on him what he had done to this other human being. The other member did survive. McCall was convicted, sent to prison as a hard offender, and to a group of cons. In prison, there was a discussion group, talking about philosophy and ethics. This was the first time he had talked seriously with people who knew about this field. Little by little he changed. He began living his life and education in prison and post-prison, then eventually became a journalist for the *Washington Post*.

McCall then wrote this book. He was not leading a psychopathic life pattern. For me, it raises the question of how good a job we do with those people from that background. We discount our understanding of people from the ghetto.

A member of the group asked whether McCall had psychopathic traits which would indicate a severe lack in his character. That is central to the issue of understanding his motivation towards crime and his treatment. He held that if one does master a particular problem, it will continue in a life of crime. A member was struck by the high intelligence on the part of McCall. A member noted that he also stayed out of the gang and then went on to state how he got caught. I cited Aichhorn's experience in *Wayward Youth* with members of his "gang." Another member stated that he had worked with gang leaders and noted they had loyalties and concern for others. The concept of the gang as family arose. The group moved on to consider the social aspect of the aberrant family system, illustrated with the ceremonies of the Masai in Kenya relative to the assumption of manhood.

For me there were intriguing parallels. From time to time I have read about Masai in Kenya. They have a strong cultural pattern that a child is a child until puberty, when at that point they are made into warriors, blood brothers, and not eligible to marry. They have their own laws and creed. A member cited "if you put him in Dr. Abrahams' place he will die in a week", an intriguing parallel between that pattern and that in urban areas. Bonding leading to the adaptation in the course of puberty. We diagnose and treat in accordance with middle-class acculturation.

The original presenter stated we do our own efforts to turn them into middle-class, mindful persons. The value above all was that you stick to whatever it is that you're supposed to be and do. A member volunteered that excitement was central to that identity.

Another member cited that Dr. Meloy, a contributor to the field, emphasized the latter as a component of the psychopathology. I noted that one encounters depression on the part of the subject when one accesses them through empathy; our middle-class values get in the way. Finding their way out of the morass is possible for them once they peel away levels of their defenses. The presenter noted that when they are adapted to their culture, they recognize no awareness of disturbance, they consider themselves to be healthy. A member cited that many of our patients do well in south-central Los Angeles.

The presenter emphasized the need for an adequate level of intelligence on the part of a Masai warrior. He noted that an integrated culture has a low crime rate. The Aboriginal culture of Australia, surviving in a very harsh environment, has no crime rate or concept of it.

A member formulated that Atascadero State Hospital bridges cultures, versus a liberal takeover, in doing so creating the possibility of lasting health rather than conforming to middle class stereotypes. The seminar ended on the note that McCall was influenced by his prison discussion group, which bridges cultures philosophically, to seek an identity and course in life that helped him realize his potential. I noted that there was a lesson in transformative idealism for us to learn, in formulating and effecting our ward programs.

June 9, 1994

The group approached the subject of the reaction of the staff to the actively violent patient as institutional countertransference. The subject was exemplified by the course of a previously violent patient who responded to therapeutic community in a positive manner. Rather than the therapeutic nihilism of prolonged isolation and intense medication, employment of therapeutic community brought this patient around. I proposed formation of a special unit composed of such patients with specially trained personnel. A corollary approach would be collegial collaboration on the part of the staff.

Members noted that the patients, while consuming an inordinate amount of attention, had previously resulted in helplessness on the part of local authority, isolation, and consequent neglect of their capacity for constructive engagement. The experience of the therapeutic community on Ward 10 with Calendar was one in which he became a pro-social leader, the opposite of his alienation and prior violence.

August 8, 1994

The next seminar dealt with the impossibilities in treatment. A member brought up experience at the beginning of his career with a patient who compulsively cut his wrists. He was addicted to barbiturates. This followed a long career in reformatories. He tore out the stitches that followed the cutting episodes. He presented a problem in management based on an apparent willingness to pay any price to get his way.

A member stated that one is helpless when one's son is persistently defiant. A member gave an example of a prisoner who stated that he had no choice but to risk death in defying authority—he "had to." A member cautioned explaining away the motivation of the patient. Members held that psychopaths in extreme form are willing to die for their cause. I at this point reported that such a patient who told me that he "had to".

In contradiction, a member cited a case of a psychopath who arrived at a pro-social, altruistic solution to his dilemmas.

There was evidence of a therapeutic alliance. This was exemplified in the case of a colleague who was honored in reconciliation on his deathbed by a prisoner of 25 years before.

Several examples of deeply resistive patients emerged in the discussion, one of whom became massively schizophrenic when he lost his psychopathic defenses. Members agreed with this, in their experience, stemming from "powerful life scripts."

Members agreed that Calendar was underneath it driven to suicide. His extreme resistance to conformity makes appearance in court impossible. I then cited the concept of "the therapeutic despair," stemming from such behavior, as indicative of an underlying intention on the part of the patient. Emancipation from fixation in that struggle is called for. A transcendent consideration there was keeping the patient alive. Members cited instances of solutions to those dilemmas in their experience.

The seminar ended on the note of Freud's Theory of the death instinct as underlying the compulsivity of the cases cited by the members. Members agreed that they had experienced enmeshment with a compulsive imperative when we felt helpless, and through that countertransference, we conceived what the transference was.

April 7, 1994

The members agreed to pursue the psychoanalytic theory of aggression. They referred to Freud's Civilization and Its Discontents, and the task of mastering the instinct for aggression and self-destruction. Aggression may be generated in reaction to frustration, developmental and adaptive, pluralistic and integrative.

In considering the death instinct, there are *Eros* and *Thanatos*. Creativity needed to be joined to aggression. Fenichel was critical of the death instinct. Hartman, Kris, and Lowenstein brought up the issue of neutralized aggression, in the integration of the ego. Waelder emphasized it as a stimulus and a threat to self-preservation. Fromm emphasized benign aggression versus malignant aggression, the human propensity to destroy and crave for absolute control. The result is a specific character disorder, necrophilia.

July 26, 1994
Sex Offenders: The Garden of Eden and Other Myths

In the following, the members associated freely on the various myths. In the Garden of Eden there was blissful union with the mother. One is prematurely expelled, trying to reconstitute this loss. The rapist is deranged consequent to this expulsion, of being cut off from that bliss.

In the bible story Lot's wife looked back, and was consumed by the sight of transgressive family disaster. Association in the group related to leaving him to have sexual activity with his daughter. A member stated "People do not see molestation until long after. Loss of love is the original castration anxiety."

The group then tackled an assortment of transgressive myths, bringing together a naked man and a similarly dark woman. This session unfortunately did not progress beyond mere mention of the vast array of myth and vision at its beginning. This would have called for Dr. Saunders and myself to have taken hold and guided the group toward their systematic exploration. Instead, we followed a laissez-faire format.

January 30, 1995
The Therapeutic Alliance and Measuring the Product

Following is a summary of the conversation during this important meeting:

Is therapeutic community necessary? Can the hospital do without it? Do we want them here as patients or prisoners? A member stated it is most important to give care. Another member stated that the answer involves change from institution to individual.

The problems are that to engage on a one-to-one basis would exceed the capacity of care of the hospital. So if we need such a therapeutic alliance, then it is an issue of what type. In transforming it into a hospital from a prison, one needs to account for the roles and capacity called for in leadership towards that end. The medical director stated that in his practice he emphasized the importance that both patients and staff have confidence in themselves. He had achieved his goal of their capacity to do fine when he went away. I cited that I didn't do anything special to Valliant in the therapeutic alliance. I do get them to cooperate; the ward plays a role in that. Pertinent there is the bond formed between staff and patients that sustains the unit. That as an example of the therapeutic alliance on Ward 24, I treated the patient Valliant as I did any other on the ward, in the special way I did the others on Ward 24.

Dr. Saunders then stated: "We don't have to have transference to have the therapeutic alliance. It is possible to have a benign alliance that stays away from the transference. We can be like surgeons and don't have to have them open up. That's one of the weaknesses of our discipline in this setting." At this time, we lacked study of that issue.

The Medical Director stated that we have an assumption that if people are getting along better, it could be from a better frame of mind. That's the notion of social disruption. He noted that Eric Berne describes the games people play in manipulating situations, one can imply a sense of gain there. We are not manipulating but educating the patient on the trial competency unit. Here we seek to instruct the patients to prepare for their roles in court.

The medical director stated his belief that the well-being of the patient is of the foremost interest. We are in *loco parentis*, as agents of society and taking care of our charges. Our job is the change of self-concept and position in society. In prescription of medication to the psychotic and psychopathic patient, we change their chemistry, whether they like it or not. There is an aggressive chemical; then there was serotonin. We look forward to therapy of the very genes in the future. Concerning psychological tests, the ASP test of orientation and attitude carried a certain amount of validity. I stated we can certainly start from that point. A member then called attention to the existence of the underlying natural instinct. As advances in nationwide treatment parameters emerge, the hospital engages with them.

The discussion moved to the resources devoted to the maintenance of the patients' well-being: just 20% of its resources. The Medical Director posited there is a question of enlisting those resources in psychoanalysis. He went on to exert that he believed in bio-psychosocial rehabilitation which is an attempt to change the individual and its group, utilizing biologic, psychological and social theory. I then stated there is no contradiction between psychoanalysis and bio-psychosocial rehabilitation: psychoanalysis is based on instincts and the psychology of the individual and their group from a dynamic point of view. Psychoanalysis penetrates more deeply into myth and a concept of the specific evolution and maturation of the individual, plus resolution of internal conflict. Finally I cited that without the alliance we were merely manipulating the patients.

The members set forth a future goal relative to measurement. This seminar had varied in size from 5 to 25 members of the staff and in the depth and pertinence of its inquiry. The psychoanalytic members had achieved exposition of their approach to rehabilitation of the psychopath. The seminar as a whole had just begun the problem in theoretic and operational terms in a dialectic exemplified by the medical director.

We did not even broach the topic of the quality circle movement and its mathematic emphasis. The members did agree on the importance of consensus/dissensus on theoretic and operational issues.

CHAPTER VI

Pastoral Collaboration

I discovered, at the inception of my work with the severely disordered at Fort Knox, a central factor in the conversion of committed psychopaths to collaborative rehabilitees. My therapeutic associates and I discerned that factor to be messianism on my and their part which enabled the prisoners to make that transition. We also discovered that messianism to be inherent in the nascent professional identity of the therapist when they were conducting their groups. Further inquiry brought out that the rehabilitees exhibited a sense of loss of their previous state of superiority as psychopaths, resulting in headaches, confusion, depression, and abdominal discomfort of psychosomatic origin. This in turn brought the rehabilitee to sick-call and conference with the attending physician on their symptomology. They soon recovered as they became acclimated to their new reality.

I did not have the wit or initiative at that time to consult with the Protestant minister who served the Fort Knox rehabilitation center concerning this profound spiritual experience. War's end left me with the desire to clear up the matter. In the context of the range of disciplines participating in the group treatment program; psychiatry, social work, psychology, education, dance therapy, nursing, and psychodrama. Later in my career I was brought into collaboration with the Protestant and Catholic ministers at St. Elisabeth's.

More than that I had the responsibility of conducting what came to be called professional identity group analysis with the pastoral trainees. The Protestant minister at St. Elisabeth's, Reverend David Dod, discussed what would be happening to his trainees as they became intimate with the secular trainees—psychiatric, psychological, et cetera. Along the way he proposed a think tank to concentrate on the subject of pastoral care and psychiatry. It is of note that he grew doubtful to the point of calling his trainees out of the general group work training program.

During his affiliative phase, he touted the work at St. Elisabeth's to the general pastoral community in Washington, D.C., resulting in an invitation on the part of the Pastoral Institute of Greater Washington for collaboration. They had a task which centered on mastering the dyadic and procedures for groups of troubled couples. The work eventuated in a large-scale pastoral care and counseling endeavor, involving a number of ministries, mostly Anglican, in the Washington area. Reverend Charles Jaekle was the chief organizer there. He, his colleagues, and I affiliated in the close fashion that I came to experience later with Reverend David Dod and also with Father Walsh, cited in this volume. They did not shy away from the concept and practice of messianism nor from my formulation of the phenomenon of what I came to call my "Intuitometer." In fact, Reverend Jaekle and his group helped me arrive at that neologism.

On leaving Washington and seeking further immersion in standard psychoanalysis, I left these matters behind, but they came to the floor in later work with a floridly psychotic patient, who called for full engagement of my messianism and Intuitometer. Along the way in my practice I had achieved analysis of deeply narcissist individuals who had regressed or progressed as the case might be into Godhead status. These individuals traversed a highly dramatic crisis of transferential nature in which deep in their soul they ascertained contact with the introjected parent to whom they were attached to with bonds of fealty. That traversal allowed them to mourn the introject and the attendant life circumstance, such fixation had deprived them of. It was doubtful whether I was able to analyze the messianism which gave me entrée to such depth psychology. I decided prior to retirement to test out my hypotheses in the context of a maximum-security mental institution analogous to those experienced early in my career. Resident at Atascadero State Hospital were two pastoral care professionals, Father Vincent Walsh and Reverend David Dod. I sought their counsel in collaboration as I encountered spiritually relevant challenges.

Early in my work at ASH as chair of the department of psychiatry I was called on to deal with a patient who despite medication sang out night and day, "I am Satan, I am Satan!" On the face of it this called for exorcism, and I called on Father Walsh for understanding relative to the solution of this problem. Expecting him to come out with religious atonements and laying on of hands, lighting of candles, et cetera, he addressed the patient in ordinary tones relative to what the patient was going through and how he felt about himself. That was what I would have done at the inception of the interview in just that manner. The patient responded immediately, informing us that he had been going through a rough time and appreciated our help. He sat up and further thanked us. The inference I drew was the one that I had early in my career relative to my subjective state while leading psychopathic groups, in which the thought as a voice in my head appeared, "These are my people." I realized then a connection to my youth in which I sought affiliation with an Irish gang on the Lower East Side that was intent on demonstrating its masculinity. I inferred that Father Walsh was undergoing an analogous experience with this errant Catholic and knew the way back to his deity. Father Walsh and I struck up a very close collaboration and friendship that continued until his death years later.

While walking the halls of ASH with Father Walsh, I was witness to his response to the call for consultation by patients in transit and his remarkable capacity to transact with them on their spiritual level. A normalizing effect was manifest there, of impressive nature.

On the basis of a particular session with Father Walsh in which we were able to jointly experience and confirm the patient Valliant's messianism and increasingly evident Satanism. It is as follows:

Pastoral Interview with Vincent Walsh

June 8, 1994 –

DR. ABRAHAMS: I see you as a deeply religious person, who is disillusioned and bitter.

WALSH: Just where do you rest, in that regard?

VALLIANT: I get mad at God.

WALSH: You seek God, yet feel abandoned and betrayed.

VALLIANT: I feel abandoned and betrayed.

WALSH: You feel the Almighty is playing a game with you.

VALLIANT: I am not Peter, but Paul.

DR.ABRAHAMS: He is testing me all the time.

WALSH: Your life is filled with tests.

VALLIANT: They put me in an institution at 6.

WALSH: Who?

VALLIANT: My mother did. She did for kids who did not have a home.

WALSH: Was she homeless?

VALLIANT: She could not live there. She never said why, I just assumed.

WALSH: You felt neglected and abandoned.

VALLIANT: So they said. In the apartment, I did not eat for three days. No one was there.

WALSH: You have brothers and sisters?

VALLIANT: They separated us right away. They put me and Mike with a black family. Scott and Elizabeth. . .

WALSH: Did you ever see them?

VALLIANT: After five years. It was not easy for me to adapt. I was a little monster. At seven, I declared this boy definitely insane he ran up and down the hall, slamming doors, making noise, noise. I was on medication at an early age.

WALSH: What medications?

VALLIANT: Dilantin, Thorazine. I slept easy because of the Thorazine. I have been on psychotropic drugs almost all my life. At that time I hadn't adjusted to them, like now. They dope me up and I slobbered. I was very angry and rageful. They had to hold me down.

DR. ABRAHAMS: Did you ever cry?

VALLIANT: I screamed and also cried. Then my foster father separated me from the other kids. I then slept in the backyard and in a sleeping bag. There was a fence around me. I drank out of the dog dish. I was blaming God at that point. Then in the institution, Ms. Keller read the Bible about Jesus every night. I knew that he was a real prodigal, would get me to my brothers. He answered me. My foster father had put me in a box and locked me in. The police took me to juvenile hall. A year before, I was with my mother.

WALSH: Did you see them?

VALLIANT: She took me home for Christmas for a week and she gave me a fire truck.

Commentary

Father Walsh and I assumed that in Valliant's messianic identity that he had a deep personal relationship with God. I thought that his regression in which he became what he called a little monster, was a bottoming out from that belief. He hints at a similar identity on the part of his mother, with her taking care of homeless children, yet farming out her own. Manifesting that of a professional who neglect their own, while devoting themselves to the care of others.

Then the story goes deeply regressive, reaching its apogee when this wild child made his foster father treat him like an animal, and he was saved by the police, through institutionalization. By then, his alienated identity had taken hold. His argument with God is reflective of his mother's devotion to Him, and her Christ-like role in his life.

This episode engaged in as a consultation on my part evidently served to strengthen the spiritual component of the therapeutic alliance. Later, I found it necessary to engage with another pastoral individual for the analysis of the messianism and Satanism Father Walsh and I had encountered.

I became convinced of the need for pastoral collaboration, when it came to deeper analytic work with the patient. In the course of the work on this deeply troubled man's very soul, I called on Reverend David Dod. My reason for such evocation was my sense that patient Valliant was deeply invested in a messianic capacity that would take extensive analysis. Reverend Dod's matter-of-fact mode of conduct of his role and capacity could serve as a platform for such analysis. This estimate proved to be true as we went along in our work together, the patient, Reverend Dod and I. A further summary of our work with him follows. On March 13, 1995 Reverend Dod became a significant feature in the treatment. The consequent sessions in detail can be found in Appendix B, section B3.

In the initial establishment of the therapeutic alliance between the doctor and Valiant, the patient entered into a reverie, prominently spiritual and ultimately related to his symbiosis with his mother. Valliant also professed a "Fear of the Unknown" which alerted the doctor to a potentially religious issue. The mysterious unknown had an enigmatic quality. In the second treatment session on May 22nd 1995 I had suspected that this patient was his mother's "Jesus," as evidence by his professed capacity to argue with God. Based upon my previous experience with pastoral matters, in which I had engaged intimately with a range of ministers, chiefly Reverend Bruder and Walsh.

By the fourth session patient Valliant manifested a state of deep reflection, akin to the free association in psychoanalysis. In addition it took on a spiritual dimension. His cognitive capacity was intact relative to what he called, "the seeds of his troubles." He also had learned to abstain from his previous vicious temper, evoked in parlance by his fellow patients. He was aware of the state of his soul in which Christ was by his side. The inward struggle between his heart's love for God while his mind underwent profound "drainage" by despair. Patient was struck by deep boredom which blocked his prayers. This had resulted in a significant break from school and work, which as the patient stated was paradoxically relieved by alcohol. Valliant's mother had worshipped the ground he had walked on and chose at this point to abandon him. As a token to troubles to come she slapped him as she commissioned him to take care of the family. In the previous self-inquiry of treatment with another psychiatrist the patient experienced a regression to a feral state and also an epileptiform spell, accompanied by awareness of being his own judge and executioner. The therapist increasing became aware of the depth of this man's spiritual disturbances.

Then the patient opened up about a subjective feeling of not being able to go on with his life. This evidence of despair turned out to be spiritually related. Dod interpreted this as evidence of the patient's alienation from self. The next phenomenon in this man's spiritual journey was a report in a group therapy session by hearing his name being called by the deity. He then revealed a mélange of memories attendant to a Job-like desire to cry. This was followed by the report of a loss of belief in his mother and the deity, and the assumption of universal guilt. Valliant then spoke of a wish for reconciliation with his family. At the same time this was marked by an especially strong intuitive connectedness with the doctor. At this point the patient entered into a crucial phase in the work. He experienced a subjective loss of his pedestal position within himself and awareness that it stemmed from his special position with his mother early in life.

The following sessions are summaries which were selected specifically because of the interaction with Reverend Dod and were interspersed between Valliant's two and a half years of his succeeding treatment.

Pastoral Consultation Summaries

May 11, 1995 – Reverend Dod discerned that the patient felt abandoned by God and left spiritless. The doctor inferred that the patient had become alienated from his internal Godhead. Reverend Dod also estimated that the patient had lost faith in the provident deity. At issue there was his inherent Godhood and the one he incorporated from his mother.

May 15, 1995 – Patient agreed with Reverend Dod's inference that the deity was set against him. The doctor, minister, and the patient arrived a state of deep despair, searching for basic belief in existence and providence.

June 1, 1995 – In the next session Reverend Dod suggested allowing the Godhead to help oneself, a transaction analogous to that in AA of opening oneself to the higher power. Along with that the Doctor in his analytic stance called on the patient to exercise his inherent capacity to inquire into his situation in-depth. Reverend Dod while devote in his religious affirmations additionally shares this empirical stance.

June 6, 1995 – The three members of this group were by evidence and honesty simple human beings to their conceived Godhead. At core there is their simple humanity. In yielding his initiative relative to a writ of *habeas corpus* Valliant is trusting in this minister and doctor for a solution of his dilemma. He cited his belief in Christian philosophy and practice while the doctor cited that as affirmation beyond usual human capacity. The conversation then moved over to the belief system of the patient and minister. The minister attested to a central change since his childhood, that of abandonment of the view of predestination. He made this change, in favor a capacity for self-initiative and overall inclusiveness. Patient began expounding on the issue of the end of days and resurrection. Dod called an authoritarian voice on the radio citing the ends of days into question. Dod also asserts the relative overall authority of the Bible concerning man's right to his own mind. The patient then brought up his experience of being in a dark tunnel and the issue of his hope for himself. Then the discussion moved over to Reverend Dod and his personal report on his parents aging spirituality as they move towards death and his consonance with them. They are moving towards a mutually determined tolerant spirituality, analogous to that of Christ. This attainment of simple humanity by this triad marked a seminal point in the treatment. At core was the recognition of abstinence from Godhood status. Pertinent there was the myth of Narcissus in which Tyrese, the ancient one, cited to the mother of Narcissus that when her son got to know himself he would die. Narcissus there was seeking in the waters more than an object of admiration, but attainment of his true identity that was as a human being as differentiated from the Godhood he enacted as an Olympian. It is to be noted that Narcissus was the issue of the river God, who had copulated with a mortal maiden.

June 15, 1995 – At this point in the account the doctor experienced what he calls his "Intuitometer" marking his deep intuitive connectedness with material amounting to a mortal wound. In his account patient cites being taken in by the Baptist church after being abandoned by his mother. She was to return after two weeks but never did. In the gradual realization of such there was an awareness of its spiritual implication. He then assiduously searched the Bible in the book of Revelations for answers. Thereupon enacting aspects of the devil.

June 22, 1995 – Both the doctor and minister in this account failed in a primary task, evidence of empathic identification with this sufferer. Later on in the treatment in regard to attestation of injustice the patient reported the assumption of the role of "avenger." This relates to the current sessions theme of injustice, first detailing the 147 days he was physically restrained to keep him from physical punishment of himself and others. He also denoted the lack of effective treatment, with transferring units as the only solution. The latter concerned the anguish of his mother never returning.

June 25, 1995 – Patient cited his insomnia as related to the avoidance of mourning relative to his personal loss. At this point in therapy Valliant was beginning to mend sundered relations with his immediate family.

June 29, 1995 – Patient was alluding to things rather than denotation, he covered a more intellection versed fashion of the role of the hospital in his life. He detailed his growing maturity and how he feels more prepared for a possible transfer.

July 6, 1995 – Revisited rape scene, domination through bite of breast, in context of addiction with maternal underlayment. This patient attest that he could not pin down why he bit this woman's breasts. One can infer that he had struggles with his mother prior to leaving the family in which he had tantrums. From his previous material centering on oral issues one can further infer that the biting on the woman was related previous unrelated issues with his mother. Assimilation through reliving and self-acceptance in the context of acceptance by therapists. Adducing his God-like status with his mother one can infer she and it belonged to him.

July 13, 1995 – Patient seeks redemption for wishing to heal the pain he had inflicted. Prayerful communion, regarding the patient's deepest soul aspirations and his attendant guilt. He sees himself to be the lowest and most reviled of creatures.

July 10, 1995 – Tobacco was his God, breaking from him. He was thrown into the river by people who did unto him. He goes on to cite further data on how his peers attempted to humiliate him in a deathly fashion and his internal resolve as punisher to kill them. It is likely at that point that Valliant entered a career as punisher, taking a bizarre form in torturing and killer animals, ultimately assaulting a woman sexually. Along the way he refers to his struggle with his addiction to pornography and wish to emancipate himself from it.

July 13, 1995 – Reverend Dod addresses the issue of self-forgiveness, with its attendant intrapsychic struggle with his internal Godhead and its standards. At core the session involved a prayerful communion, involving deep intuitive connectedness regarding the patient's deepest soul aspirations and his attendant guilt.

August 29, 1995 – He made contact with his alienated evil identity, regressing to feral self-images as a snake, visiting nadir aspects of his soul and an aspect of the Earth which would be volcanic.

September 26, 1995 – Patient no longer exhibited an explosive temper. He claimed a soul of own, was able to traverse the report of the hell of loss of mother, his nadir state, and his experience of remorse, crucifixion and after this was able to call his soul his own. In transaction with Reverend Dod relative to the patient's religious experience, patient reported, "I was enclosed, in blackness." It appeared at first that the patient was his own pastor, in equity with Christ. He called the soul his own, no longer a punitive God punishing himself.

October 12th, 1995 – Accepting the ambiguity and disorder of reality. In this mélange of feelings most significant would be the patient's experience of being haunted by his personal past. There his deviation from his internal Godhead and its significance on his relationship with his parents would be key. There is reference to internal hunger and the need to be fed. Patient gives testament to that process when he talked about unburdening himself. The doctor experienced intuitive connectedness at that point. The Godhead is now transmuted into a humane, forgiving God.

October 19th, 1995 – Relating transaction with the rehabilitation therapist is where her authentic rage and deep disappointment reached him, seeing his infantile reaction, resulting in Pruno episode, and self-sabotage.

November 29th, 1995 – This soul talk is confused, but indicative of his slow reaching to change self. His participation in the Alcoholics Anonymous is an act of humility indicative of character change.

January 3, 1996 – Patient links his sensitivity to manic states in others and self with his tie to his mother and seeing her as a separate person, demythologized. It was apparent that he is in position to analyze the myth that he had created of positive and negative sort. Dod commented, "You put yourself in your mother's shoes, and had compassion towards her, versus being angry, betrayed, and abandoned." Along with that, he appeared to be obtaining perspective on his experience of God.

January 17, 1996 – Haunted state, from boyhood, reawakened by seeing Casper and Ghost image. Inherent to the experience of ghost is that of psychic death and resurrection. Again the immediacy of this experience is attested to by his crying, "Like a baby."

January 23, 1996 – Patient in concert with Reverend Dod and the doctor attested to a state of honesty and centeredness in his very soul. He reported reaching out to his peers in a helpful fashion. Additionally, Valliant opened up in AA group regarding killing animals, mothered by the members. Patient is distancing himself from an immersion in the nightmare and heroics of the past with the attainment of a steadier self-esteem.

January 30, 1996 – The dialogue moved then hazards of a state of integrity, the pain attendant from deviation from subjective and objective, and here centering upon the experience of parting from the hospital and its human environment. Reverend Dod is quoted for saying, "People betray us, we are still able to maintain balance, versus being at their mercy. It is important being able to close doors, pain—without a tailspin." Saying "goodbye" in the past has been fraught with tremendous emotion, reflective of an infantile tie with his maternal object. He is waking to the reality of the present with its verity and its ambiguity.

February 5, 1996 – Doctor and minister are transacting with patient, alongside one another on the issue of integrity and self-maintenance, in an affirmative fashion, in the context of two stressful situations with his peers. Dod is denoted for commenting on the patient's firm flexibility rather than barreling ahead.

Unfortunately, here we come across a gap in this patient's account. This gap is reflective of lack of record, rather than lack of continuance of treatment.

September 23, 1996 – Remarkable here was this poem's here to move the doctor several decades later after the experience. Why it is denoted is because of the strong spiritual undertones.

Patient presented a poem:

MAKING AMENDS WITH THE ANIMALS

Tonight I petted you
Your fur was soft and great
Caressing him with my fingers
Took the pain away

'Till now I lived in fear
That you never could forgive
The sorrow that I gave
In the lifestyle that I lived

To steal your breath away
Again and again and again
Would Jesus ever give, forgive
This sadistic horrid sin

Will I ever let go
Of the guilt and all the shame
Or carry it forever
And continue on the same

I thank you for a creature
That God has made to love
I think that I'll just let you
And thank Jesus up above

For allowing me to touch you
It sets my spirit free
I feel your heart is something
For all eternity

So thank you for your love
I give it back to you
And I'll never ever hurt you
The way I used to do

October 2, 1996 – Patient is striving with might and main to alter his character towards normalcy. His underlying affective state eludes him and he is implicitly asking the doctor to enter it into him.

November 6, 1996 – There is anger at the loss of individuality about having to leave his self-absorption and reach out to others, also relating to a self-persecutory role.

November 13, 1996 – In this session not overtly evidencing pastoral issues, patient's liability to initiative with in his psyche, i.e., that which, "pulls the strings" resulting in facial tics is closer to the surface.

November 27, 1996 – Patient fought against his compulsive sexual drive, but does not know what inside him impels it. Does not know, but still senses an internal state arousal and impulsion by which he struggles mightily to sequester it in his psyche. Reverend Dod's formulation of Christ's internal reconciliation appears misplaced since the conflict was evidently a continuing one. The Reverend's association to President Carter's internal sexual conflict carries the inquiry a step closer to its possible consummation.

December 4, 1996 – Further data regarding sexual compulsions earlier in life, 22–23. Patient is in touch with his symbiosis regarding his maternal object and enacting with it as he analytically traverses it, letting go of it as he goes along with a hint of mourning. Valliant is also denoted for referencing scripture depicting the separation of Joseph from his family as something that was evil that God intended for good.

December 11, 1996 – Again, there is a line of mourning which appear in the midst of this semi-confession at times patient induced deep intuitive connectedness relative to his suffering. The chaos appears to be subsiding.

If pastoral care relates to the care and feeding of soul. In summary here would be that of what occurred in this man relative to his soul and its vicissitudes and that between the members of the triad, Reverend Dod Dr. Abrahams and the patient. I had found that this patient was accessible to pastoral care when I matched him with Father Walsh. Patient Valliant in an open heartened way citing his ongoing argument with God. This argument was to be the chief content with the subsequent work with Reverend Dod. In it he first announced his cognitive capacity in thinking about such matters. An earlier encounter with a staff position to help him in this regard resulted in the sudden onset of monumental confusion, terror, and emergency restitution action.

Employing large quantities of neuroleptics. An inference that I drew from this was that the messianic alliance that patient had achieved with me, Father Walsh and now Reverend Dod protected him from his massive incapacity. We then were able to proceed with an alliance that might be termed as pastoral analogous to the therapeutic alliance in psychiatry. Patient announced his wish to inquire into the "seeds of his troubles" (his troubled soul). The seeds that emerged were evidenced to exist in his relationship with his mother and the vicissitudes of her belief in him, his in himself, her belief in him as a god-like object "pedestal figure," his belief in himself appeared to be merged with her belief in him. Patient then disgorged a story a story in detail of her abandonment of him at age 6 and his consequent regression into psychosis and psychopathy in which he acted as a monster out of control and barely subject to large doses neuroleptics. From that emerged a self-concept as "punisher" of evident satanic nature.

Reverend Dod played a crucial role in engaging about his abandonment by the deity. Then remarkably in their search patient, doctor and reverend entered into a state of deep despair and David Dod led us out of it toward a state of intellectual, moral, and emotional integrity. My empiricism at that point was manifested in a call on the patient to search is soul for evidence of his Godhead. Reverend Dod then cited how he had found his own way in ecclesiastical fashion when younger, in abandoning the Presbyterian belief in predestination. Dod asserted the right to his own mind and the patient joined in on data about his own biblical research on the end of days. Doctor, patient, and the Reverend exchanged as simply human beings and in the account the Doctor cited data from Greek mythology concerning Narcissus and his death when he got to know himself. Emerging from mourning patient's loss of God-like status with his mother, Valliant began analysis of his avenger role and his sadistic bite of his victim's breast.

177

Concerning the issue of remorse Reverend Dod then initiated discussion related to forgiveness in prayerful enactment. In transacting with Reverend Dod patient in Christ-like fashion reported he was able to call his soul his own for the first time. Patient then unburdened himself about the haunt of the past, in which abandonment by his mother had been accompanied by self-abandonment of his own Godhead. This was accompanied by internal hunger and the need to be fed. Midway through sessions with Dod patient reported how reconciled he felt to a rehabilitation therapist who soulfully had berated him for his failure to live up to their agreed upon ideal. He next shared what came to be acknowledged as a mythology, positive and negative concerning his mother, a process Reverend Dod cited as putting himself in his mother's shoes and accepting her as a separate person. Patient broached parapsychological experience of ghosts, coupled with unaccountably mourning his past.

Additionally, Reverend Dod played a large part in giving voice to the patient's attainment of a state of firm flexibility and capacity to sustain emotional and spiritual losses. Patient at this point presented a poem ostensibly addressed to his tortured and murdered animals in which he poses his problem stemming from his tie with his maternal introject of moral bondage and violation of which earlier resulted in a state of terror and perdition. Approaching his discharge from the hospital to a less secure hospital with the prospect of continuing therapy patient in this final phase of his treatment touched on a core item his sexual tie with his mother. He had struggled to sequester in within his soul and now realized its immediacy. He vaguely related it to a facial tic that had besotted him lifelong. All of this was accompanied by incidents of mourning and steady intuitive connectedness.

It is of note that Reverend Dod grew in his participation and his comprehension of the intrapsychic struggles of this complex individuals and his capacity for initiative for carrying the triad through developmental crisis. In corollary fashion this patient assumed a ministerial function on his own of healthy sort, achieving at the end contact with the "seeds of his trouble." For the author achievement of this pastoral analysis in good part relieved him of a sense of failure he had experienced in work with a previous psychopathic patient, the one that led him to attempt the work at Atascadero State Hospital. Confirmed also was the insight in professional practice that my associates and I had achieved at Fort Knox, when we noted the centrality of messianism in the treatment of psychopathy. I was there converted to a career choice, comparable to the conversion of the psychopaths at the Fort Knox from antisocial to prosocial and to the study of that process of conversion in my subsequent career.

CHAPTER VII

Summary and Conclusions

I cite in my title, *Circles of Change: An Adventure in Therapeutic Community at Atascadero State Hospital,* its quality as an adventure. My account is replete with summaries, and a summary of those summaries is at this point hardly necessary. Then, how was this massive venture an adventure? In it, I retraced the steps of previous adventures: in my army days at Fort Knox, where we were able to reach the psychopathic offender and reverse his malign life course; in my discovery of the accessibility of the severely disordered to treatment in the maximum security section of St. Elizabeth's Hospital; in discovery of the role of messianism in my professional development and my subsequent efforts at its analysis; the adventitious treatment and training program at St. Elizabeth' Hospital, in which we trained an array of disciplines in equity to collaborate on establishment of a therapeutic community, that change from the hierarchy of the original asylum to the relative democracy of therapeutic community giving promise to the possibility and way towards institutional change elsewhere in society; and in my private practice, reaching into the massive defenses of the severely disordered and his family, employing individual analysis, group, and family therapy analytically in that regard.

All of those developments came into application in my work at ASH, and were the lessons learned at St. Elizabeth's applied in thoroughgoing fashion to the problems at ASH, we could have developed a comparable training and treatment program. Instead, I was able to do so to an extent on two wards and engage with the general staff for the rest of the hospital in a series of colloquia with Dr. David Saunders. With Dr. Saunders, I conducted a para-educational seminar on psychoanalysis with the psychiatric staff, itself in preparation for a planned group treatment program. In terms of the hospital's autonomous effort at self-transmutation toward therapeutic ends, it, under the leadership of Robert Behan, had organized a treatment improvement project. This body consisted of departmental heads and/or their representatives, had surveyed the therapeutic programs each had been mounting, and engaged in a collaborative effort at forging a new therapeutic paradigm. Under my instance, this would culminate in a group work training program, modelled after the one I had initiated at St. Elizabeth's earlier in my career. A decision at the State Department of Mental Hygiene aborted this effort, in favor of one at transmuting management of the hospital in accordance with the Quality Circle model.

I joined the ranks of a venture mandated by the State of California in retraining the staff in alteration of management to deepen it psychoanalytically, following the initiatives developed in Japan by W. Edwards Deming. There Deming and his followers had applied statistical analysis to the group dynamics that had appeared on the management scene mid-century. This adventure, though falling short, had helped me clarify the issues in institutional self-transformation and therapeutic trans-formation called for in the treatment of the severe disorders. I have attempted to in narrative fashion denote my experience, culminating in the appendices which hold detailed exposition of session protocols. The devil in therapy lies in this conceptual base, but also in the accuracy of the details of its experience. Both the therapeutic theory and the details are presented to the average reader, but more so to the serious student, in volume two. To aid that student, an extensive glossary is presented, as well as an annotated bibliography, both as part of this first volume.

During and towards the end of my tenure at ASH, I reached into conceptions of an ideal treatment institution of forensic nature, self-transforming and ultimately transformed. It would be situated closer to the home of the patient to afford ready visits with the family. It would be related to academia, to provide training of its professional components in their careers along the way. Additionally, it would have an ongoing relationship with the various media to afford it and society appropriate transparency. Importantly, there would be a research and development component at core, assuming a leadership role there and coordinated with academia. I would expect that as it developed, it would turn into a University within walls, and as such, its security provisions would depend upon its scrupulous adherence to its professional mis-sion, along with that of an advanced prison. Central to the paradigm of intramural forensic treatment is the concomitance of therapy and security; the therapeutic community and a sophisticated, modern prison.

Factoring in these issues of treatment, security, and administration, results, to my mind, in an institution situated in an urban setting for access to family and society. Its architecture would reflect its institu-tional requirements, yet be home-like. A minimum size to factor in basic requirements, such as the manpower needed to take down an out of control individual, an appropriately sized treatment team, a sufficient array of disciplines, as well as housekeeping and other maintenance staff. A rough estimate would indicate about 150 patients to 700 staff members as a reasonable ratio to achieve maximum efficiency. Dr. Rood, in his calculations, made room for 1,000 patients and about 1,700 personnel, and situated ASH in a more suburban setting, somewhat difficult to reach.

An issue in provision of design of this institution would be the opportunity for professional advancement of staff in their disciplines, as well as for patients in the realm of occupations and professions. The question arises: in its advancement and self-transmutation, would it phase itself out of its rationale for existence? Such would be highly unlikely. Instead, its putative success would lead to demands for its replication and eventually to its incorporation as a national institute of joint forensic and mental health nature. Group and individual analysis of patient James Valliant yielded data concerning his profound alienation from self, deep and malignant regression, then, through psychoanalytic and pastoral treatment, of a way back to himself, his family and society, and as importantly, data concerning his intrapsychic and interpersonal life, attendant theory, and optimal modes of practice. This depth of analysis could well be a goal in our future forensic facilities.

We got partway down the pike at St. Elizabeth's in its maximum security section, Howard Hall. Howard Hall was surround by a 35 foot concrete wall, only entered through a subterranean passage, yet its communication with the outside world was increasingly free, to the extent that the hospital asked for replication of its approach, in training and treatment. Such an ideal was later enacted at an institution called Hanbleceya by a group of dedicated professionals, who assembled a therapeutic group of families composed of severely schizophrenic members. They effected their mission within a suburban community, the families came from afar and collaborated in its governance and maintenance. All this called for scrupulously enacted leadership on the part of the team of professionals.

At the core of this approach was my application of Freud's analytic method. I called on the rehabilitees at Fort Knox to associate with him, verbally and otherwise, in good faith, appealing to the better angels of their nature. They reciprocated and, responding to an underlying messianism within my and their selves, they engaged in ultimately successful therapeutic communities. This process was repeated in other institutional settings, and to my inference, is at the core of Deming's success in institutional self-transformation, in Japan and elsewhere.

I have experienced a certain amount of success with it in grassroots politics (*Democracy from the Grassroots: A Guide to Creative Political Action*). Further details on such work within forensic settings may be found in *Turning Lives Around: Group Treatment of Military Prisoners*, in *This Way Out: A Narrative of Therapy of Sexual and Psychotic Offenders*, and in *The Messianic Imperative: Scourge or Savior*. Society is moving from concerted resistance to relative receptivity towards these initiatives currently in regards to its prison system. I have had personal experience with that resistance in the form of a killing attempt made by a patient located on the ward of a psychiatrist who was devoted to the old order based on repression. The personnel on Ward 10 at first resisted therapeutic community and its spontaneity, which might have marred the newly waxed floor. Such resistance can be expected on a massive scale when society determines politically to reform its prisons.

At that point, we will need to look to examples of success in the establishment of correctional community, itself based on initiative by psychiatry on therapeutic community. At issue will be the conversion from the old system to the new. Examples of such occurred in this volume first on Ward 10. There, the head nurse and others expressed concern for safety, namely that these changes would lead to a phase of chaos in transition to therapeutic community. Dragging the chairs into a circle was at issue there, rather than a straight line, and that dragging would mar the newly and perfectly waxed floor, product of hours of work by the devoted housekeeper. Demonstrated there was the idealism of the old prison way, exemplified elsewhere in society by armies and clergy. Resistance, therefore, involves all parties to the system, backed by their idealism and its correlate potential for malevolence and subversion.

Conception, evocation, and communication of the ideals of the new way called for scrupulous and effective leadership, in which all parties would be mobilized to "keep their eyes on the prize," on a continuing basis. Such leadership, present in abundance at the beginning of my career, was spotty at Atascadero State Hospital and at the state level. Colonel Miller's influence, attitude, and orientation permeated his thousand-member center, where he was acquainted with the local level and that local level was empowered to reach both mid and top levels of command. Dr. Overholser, the superintendent at St. Elizabeth's, and Dr. Couvant, the service chief, were similarly constituted. At ASH, on both state and institutional levels, leadership was "old school," had difficulty with the lower or mid-levels. On the contrary, on the ward level, the institutional therapeutic community there at ASH was central to that endeavor, in which there was a daily orientation to these matters on part of personnel and patients. Attendance to the details of this orientation and reorientation has been pursued in these volumes, particularly the latter, "The Clinical Data in Detail." The revolution in management of the Quality Circle movement somehow did not reach the clinical level of functioning at ASH, which in time regressed to its previous state.

For success in the reform of our far-flung prison system, extensive planning would be essential, as well as rigorous executive oversight to enable the participants to maintain the proper perspective, in order to avoid chaos and its attendant dangers. The baby steps that we made at ASH warrant further study to enable the reformists to more surely engage larger populations. I am reminded of a conference that I had with Colonel Miller, commandant of the Fort Knox Rehabilitation Center for Military Prisoners. We were on route to Fort Leavenworth to a convention of army prison personnel, which had the task of assembling lessons learned and planning for the future of American prison. Colonel Miller and I addressed ourselves to the composition and motivation of the new army of prison reformists, in which we were acknowledged to be in the vanguard. We felt humbled and invigorated in the process. It is in that light that these volumes are launched on the sea of American intuitional history.

In the appendix, there is a concentration on the clinical data experienced on Ward 10 and then on Ward 24. In both, the evolution of the therapeutic community is described, denoting the stages of development, accompanied by a running commentary. A special feature of the work on Ward 24 was the collaboration with Reverend David Dod, reported verbatim. This work went to the intrapsychic heart of the matter: the patient's spiritual malevolence, and the crises traversed in reconciliation with his own godhead.

In sum, the institutions cited in this volume took on the task of self-transformation. It was a task of peril but also of great promise that reached into the souls of the participants. It was a challenge engaged in by humanity since the great enlightenment in the 18th century. Viewed in a larger frame of history, we have made progress sufficient to glimpse the possibilities that the patients and personnel in these volumes envisioned. This volume is dedicated to the great adventurers Colonel Miller, August Aichhorn and Sigmund Freud who have set us on a path of personal and social transformation. It is my hope that this volume has similarly encouraged you the reader to join forces with others and form your own circles of change.